Organic Foods

by Debra A. Miller

LUCENT BOOKS
A part of Gale, Cengage Learning

Detroit • New York • San Francisco • New Haven, Conn • Waterville, Maine • London

© 2008 Gale, a part of Cengage Learning

For more information, contact:
Lucent Books
27500 Drake Rd.
Farmington Hills, MI 48331-3535
Or you can visit our Internet site at gale.cengage.com

LIBRARY OF CONGRESS CATALOGING-IN-PUBLICATION DATA

Miller, Debra A.
 Organic foods / by Debra A. Miller.
  p. cm. -- (Hot topics)
 Includes bibliographical references and index.
 ISBN 978-1-59018-994-8 (hardcover)
  1. Natural foods--United States--Juvenile literature. 2. Natural foods industry--United
States--Juvenile literature. I. Title.
 TX369.M55 2008
 641.3'02--dc22
                                                                    2007035909

ISBN-10: 1-59018-994-9

Printed in the United States of America
2 3 4 5 6 7 12 11 10 09 08

CONTENTS

FOREWORD

Young people today are bombarded with information. Aside from traditional sources such as newspapers, television, and the radio, they are inundated with a nearly continuous stream of data from electronic media. They send and receive e-mails and instant messages, read and write online "blogs," participate in chat rooms and forums, and surf the Web for hours. This trend is likely to continue. As Patricia Senn Breivik, the dean of university libraries at Wayne State University in Detroit, states, "Information overload will only increase in the future. By 2020, for example, the available body of information is expected to double every 73 days! How will these students find the information they need in this coming tidal wave of information?"

Ironically, this overabundance of information can actually impede efforts to understand complex issues. Whether the topic is abortion, the death penalty, gay rights, or obesity, the deluge of fact and opinion that floods the print and electronic media is overwhelming. The news media report the results of polls and studies that contradict one another. Cable news shows, talk radio programs, and newspaper editorials promote narrow viewpoints and omit facts that challenge their own political biases. The World Wide Web is an electronic minefield where legitimate scholars compete with the postings of ordinary citizens who may or may not be well-informed or capable of reasoned argument. At times, strongly worded testimonials and opinion pieces both in print and electronic media are presented as factual accounts.

Conflicting quotes and statistics can confuse even the most diligent researchers. A good example of this is the question of whether or not the death penalty deters crime. For instance, one study found that murders decreased by nearly one-third when the death penalty was reinstated in New York in 1995. Death penalty supporters cite this finding to support their argument that the existence of the death penalty deters criminals from committing murder. However, another study found that states without the death penalty have murder rates below the national average. This study is cited by opponents of capital punishment, who reject the claim that the death penalty deters murder. Students need context and clear, informed discussion if they are to think critically and make informed decisions.

The Hot Topics series is designed to help young people wade through the glut of fact, opinion, and rhetoric so that they can think critically about controversial issues. Only by reading and thinking critically will they be able to formulate a viewpoint that is not simply the parroted views of others. Each volume of the series focuses on one of today's most pressing social issues and provides a balanced overview of the topic. Carefully crafted narrative, fully documented primary and secondary source quotes, informative sidebars, and study questions all provide excellent starting points for research and discussion. Full-color photographs and charts enhance all volumes in the series. With its many useful features, the Hot Topics series is a valuable resource for young people struggling to understand the pressing issues of the modern era.

INTRODUCTION

ORGANIC GOES MAINSTREAM

Once confined to health food stores and favored mostly by hippies or health fanatics, organic food in recent years has experienced rapid growth. Although the organic market still represents only about 2.5 percent of the total retail food sales in the United States, the organic market has grown at the rate of about 15 to 20 percent each year into a $15 billion industry. This expanding interest in organics is not limited to the United States; organic food is also booming in European countries such as Germany, Britain, Italy, and France, and gaining acceptance around the world. In addition, some developing countries such as China, Brazil, and Uruguay have become important producers of organic crops. Many experts see no limits to the expansion of the organic industry.

An Interest in Health

The growing popularity of organic foods has been driven largely by increasing consumer interest in diets that promote health, prevent disease, and protect the environment. Supporters say organic foods are healthier and better for the environment because they are not grown with chemical fertilizers or pesticides or other ingredients believed to be toxins. Indeed, as food marketing consultant Laurie Demeritt points out, "The word 'organic' has become synonymous with 'health' and 'healthier lifestyle.'"[1] In fact, consumer demand for organic products doubled between 2000 and 2006, and according to the Food Marketing Institute, more than half of American consumers buy organic food at least once a month. And an increasing number

Organic foods are no longer sold just at farmers' markets and small health food stores. As this sign shows, they are now being sold in mainstream grocery stores throughout the United States.

of Americans—as many as 10 percent—are buying only organic produce.

As a result of this strong consumer demand, organic foods are no longer sold only at farmers' markets and small health food stores; now, they can also be found in large natural food stores and mainstream supermarkets throughout the United States. Beginning in 2000, more organic food was purchased in regular supermarkets than in any other type of retail outlet. Experts say the biggest obstacle preventing more people from buying organic foods tends to be price. Currently, most organic fruits and vegetables cost between 10 and 30 percent more than conventionally grown produce. Frozen, processed, and animal organic products can cost even more, sometimes 50 to 100 percent more than their non-organic counterparts. To respond to this concern, a number of mainstream grocers, such as Safeway and Costco, have begun to develop their own private label organic products and offer somewhat lower prices than those charged in natural food markets.

The Wal-Mart Factor

Perhaps the biggest recent development in the organic food market, however, was Wal-Mart's announcement in 2006 that it would expand its stock of organic foods and price its organic food only 10 percent above the prices of non-organic produce. Wal-Mart has been extremely successful at buying items in bulk from around the world and then selling them at bargain prices. Its supercenter stores added some organic items to their shelves about five years ago, but Wal-Mart's 2006 decision to increase organic sales, experts say, means the company is betting that it can duplicate its bargain marketing strategy in the organic food market.

Wal-Mart's entry into organic food sales is expected to further boost the sales of organic food, but it also has stirred up controversy. Some commentators welcomed the announcement, believing that it would be good for the organic market. As Natural Life magazine explained, "Wal-Mart's economy of scale will lead to greater accessibility and lower prices for consumers of organic foods...[and] increased demand...for organic farmers and processors."[2] Others criticized the Wal-Mart development as a threat to the quality of organic foods. Wal-Mart's practices of using global supply sources and transporting food for long distances, critics say, will skirt and possibly weaken national organic standards, and hurt the environment by increasing carbon emissions that cause global warming. Wal-Mart is also expected to rely on large corporate farm sources for its organic products, making the market more competitive for the small farmers and retailers who first developed the organic market. As Ronnie Cummins, director of the Organic Consumers Association, has explained, "With Wal-Mart and other folks jumping in, what will happen down the road is the small- and medium-size operators will be forced out of business."[3]

Since Wal-Mart's 2006 announcement, critics have found even more reasons for concern as reports surfaced about possible fraudulent marketing practices. A September 2006 re-

The superstore, Wal-Mart, has been charged by the Cornucopia Institute, a farm policy group, with misleading customers into believing that some foods are organic when they are not.

port from the Cornucopia Institute, a Wisconsin-based farm policy group, for example, charged that Wal-Mart is misleading consumers into believing some foods are organic when they're not. The group monitored organic food in Wal-Mart stores around the country and found numerous produce and other items in sections of the store labeled as "organic" that were not really organic. Cornucopia filed a complaint with the U.S. Department of Agriculture (USDA), but so far no action has been taken against the company.

Organics at a Crossroads

Some observers believe that the Wal-Mart news is part of a major trend that could eventually transform the organic market. Once produced by family farms and small producers who guarded organic purity, protected the environment, and treated farm animals with great respect, organic food may soon be just another corporate commodity. As Diane Brady, Associate Editor of Business Week magazine, warns:

> As food companies scramble to find enough organically grown ingredients, they are inevitably forsaking the pastoral ethos [rural character] that has defined the organic lifestyle. For some companies, it means keeping thousands of organic cows on industrial-scale feedlots. For others, the scarcity of organic ingredients means looking as far afield as China, Sierra Leone, and Brazil—places where standards may be hard to enforce, workers' wages and living conditions are a worry, and...increased farmland sometimes comes at a cost to the environment.[4]

Today, commentators agree that the organic market is at a crossroads, its future path uncertain. Ironically, many people fear that the very qualities that made organic food important to consumers—its purity and ecological values—may ultimately be diluted or lost.

THE MEANING OF "ORGANIC"

Until very recently, the term "organic" referred simply to a preference for fresh, locally-produced fruits and vegetables, grown with minimal chemical fertilizers and pesticides. Organic producers were limited to a tiny group of small-scale farmers concerned with health, nutrition, and the environment. Now, however, the "organic" label is defined and regulated by the U.S. government, and the term organic includes a wide variety of products, in addition to fresh fruits and vegetables. Clearer standards and rising consumer dissatisfaction with conventional farming practices have contributed to a rising demand for organic food.

Rising dissatisfaction with conventional farming practices, like the use of pesticides, has contributed to an increase in the demand for organic products.

Conventional Farming Methods

Organic farming is perhaps best understood by comparing it to conventional farming, which is the method used to produce the vast majority of the foods found in local supermarkets and eaten by most Americans and people around the world. In conventional farming, also sometimes referred to as industrial farming, the goal is to squeeze as much production out of the land as possible in the most efficient way, in order to maximize profits. It is often said that organic farmers feed the soil, while conventional farmers feed the plant. This is because conventional farmers do not try to build up the soil with healthy plant nutrients for long-term crop production, but instead apply chemical fertilizers containing nutrients that the crops can utilize immediately. Other chemicals are used as herbicides and pesticides to discourage weeds, disease, and insect damage. To further increase efficiency, most conventional farms also focus on growing one or two crops, often in the same locations, year after year—a practice called monoculture. There is no effort to fit the conventional farm into the natural environment; instead, conventional farmers seek to control and alter the natural world in order to increase human food production.

THE NATURAL WAY

"Organic produce is the way food was supposed to be grown ....
It's the natural way."
                    —Josh Falk, a resident of central Oregon.

Quoted in Joseph Friedrichs, "Are Organic Products Worth The Price? Bend Catches Organic Buzz," *NewWest*, January 29, 2007. www.ewg.org/news/story.php?id=5737.

In conventional livestock, dairy, and poultry operations, animals are usually confined in crowded indoor conditions. Animals are provided with the minimum conditions necessary to keep them healthy and alive just long enough to grow and produce the products for which they are raised. Conventionally-raised animals are fed a diet of non-organic feed and given food supplements to build weight and enhance the meat product. Preventative doses of antibiotics are given to animals to fend off

Organic Standards and Farm Animals

Under the USDA organic standards, animal products such as meat, milk, and eggs must meet certain minimum requirements to win an organic label. However, critics say the government's standards are not strict enough to ensure that farm animals are raised, transported, and slaughtered in a humane way. The USDA regulations, for example, provide that animals must have access to the outdoors, including access to pasture for ruminant (cud-chewing) animals such as cattle and sheep. Critics say opening a barn door just minutes per day, however, might meet this definition and organic animals may never get to roam freely around an outdoor range or pas-ture. Instead, like most conventionally raised farm animals, organically-raised animals may live in very confined, close quarters throughout their lives. To solve this problem, some animal producers are adding other labels to their foods, such as "open pasture" or "pasture-raised," to indicate that animals are raised in a pasture rather than fattened in a feedlot or confined facility. Consumers, however, must be wary of some labels that seem to suggest humane conditions; designations such as "free range," "cage-free," or "grass-fed" do not necessarily guarantee that animals are not confined or raised in the outdoors.

disease, and hormones are widely used so the animal will grow quickly and produce more meat or milk. Indeed, the typical conventional meat producer runs a very intensive factory-type operation. As David Joachim and Rochelle Davis explain:

> The vast majority of the chicken we eat today, about 98 percent, comes from large indoor poultry operations that bear more of a resemblance to factories than to our idyllic notion of farms. Within the agricultural industry, such facilities are better known by their technical name: confined (or concentrated) animal feeding operations, or CAFOs. According to the Environmental Protection Agency, poultry CAFOs house at least 100,000 broiler chickens or 55,000 turkeys on the floor of an indoor facility.[5]

The label on these eggs indicate that the chickens that produced them were organically raised by being allowed to roam freely instead of being confined in cages.

CAFOs for cattle, pigs, and other farm animals are very similar, with tens of thousands of animals packed into feedlots.

The Controversy About Conventional Farming

Conventional farming practices boost the conventional farmer's profits by increasing the amount of food produced from crops and animals. Indeed, most experts admit that conventional agriculture has achieved increasingly higher yields using these efficient, industrial techniques. The USDA, for example, states that U.S. agricultural productivity grew an average of about 1.9 percent annually between 1948 and 1999. This growth in food production, often called the "green revolution," has helped to keep food prices relatively low in the United States and in other countries that use these techniques. As a result, abundant and affordable conventional foods still make up the bulk of the U.S. and world food markets.

The conventional farming approach, however, has come under increasing criticism because of its use of massive amounts of synthetic chemical fertilizers, herbicides, and pesticides, which critics claim are dangerous to human health and bad for the environment. In addition, moral or spiritual considerations such as providing humane treatment to animals are rarely a priority for conventional farmers. As the National Center for Appropriate Technology (NCAT), a sustainable agriculture advocacy group, puts it:

> The conditions under which livestock are raised in factory farms is, to say the least, unnatural and unhealthy for the animals. Overcrowding, limited movement, lack of fresh air and sunlight, and rough handling are routine. It is a cold and cruel way to treat sentient beings.[6]

This concentrated production of animals has also been widely criticized for producing huge amounts of manure that contribute to pollution. Consumers who question the health, moral, or environmental effects of conventional agriculture are increasingly turning to organically grown food products.

The Organic Farming Approach

The difference that sets organic farmers apart from conventional farmers is a holistic approach to the land and animals that is founded, primarily, on long-term, natural processes. This approach avoids the use of synthetic chemicals, is more environmentally friendly, protects animals from inhumane treatment, and promotes biodiversity—the wide variety of plant and animal species and ecosystems typically found in nature. Organic farmers believe that respecting nature and not abusing the environment or animals enables farms to be productive for years to come—that is, be sustainable. Indeed, many organic farmers have a spiritual reverence for nature, and see their role as caretakers rather than masters of the environment. As Marsha Mason, founder of the Resting in the River Organic Farm in New Mexico, explains:

> All that we do is predicated [based] on the idea that everything is interconnected,—the earth, planets, wind, water, seeds, even rocks, and human beings and all the

other critters of the planet. Therefore everything must be respected, prayed over and worked with reverence to the holy or holistic attitude of the Golden Rule. Treat everything the way you want to be treated because God, Divine Consciousness, and Spirit exist within everything and everyone.[7]

Organic Farming Philosophies

This spiritual connection with nature is a major part of several early organic farming philosophies. One of these is biodynamic farming, an early organic system developed from lectures given in 1924 by an Austrian scientist and philosopher, Rudolf Steiner.

Biodynamic farming is an organic farming philosophy that bans the use of chemicals and promotes crop and wildlife diversity to keep pest populations in a natural balance.

Steiner rejected the use of chemical fertilizers and promoted the idea that farms must be managed as self-contained ecosystems, with attention paid not only to their biological aspects, such as soil health, but also to their place in nature. As agriculture specialist Steve Diver explains, biodynamic agriculture includes "practices [that] are intended to influence biological as well as metaphysical [spiritual] aspects of the farm, or to adapt the farm to natural rhythms (such as planting seeds during certain lunar phases)."[8]

Another well-known organic farming philosophy is called the Fukuoka method, named after Japanese soil scientist Masanobu Fukuoka, who in the early part of the twentieth century developed a type of agriculture that produced high quality fruits, vegetables, and grains without the use of plowing or tilling, chemical fertilizers or pesticides, weeding, pruning, machinery, or compost. According to Fukuoka, the purpose of farming is "to become one with nature—agriculture is an occupation in which a farmer adapts himself to nature."[9] This emphasis on cooperating with nature is at the heart of organic farming.

Organic Farming Techniques

Regardless of which particular brand of organic philosophy they might ascribe to, most modern organic farmers follow similar practices to improve and maintain the soil and deter weeds and pests. One of the most important features of organic farming is the use of natural fertilizers and methods to enrich the soil and replace the nutrients taken out by growing crops. Many organic farmers use manure from animals such as cows, chickens, and horses to supply nitrogen, one of the main requirements for all growing plants. Most organic farmers also apply compost, a rich soil additive made from decomposed organic matter (such as leaves, grass, wood chips, and straw). Compost has to be sterilized before it can be added to the soil. This is done through a carefully-controlled, heat-intensive, open-air process.

In addition to these natural methods for improving soil, organic farms sometimes use processed natural fertilizers to supply nitrogen and two other important plant nutrients—phosphorus and potassium (or potash)—as well as a variety of other important trace nutrients and minerals. These natural fertilizers include bone meal and blood meal made from animals, sea kelp from the ocean, and various mineral powders such as rock phosphate and greensand, a naturally occurring form of potash.

TURNING BACK THE CLOCK

"Certified organic farming is defined as much by what it does not accept as by what it does accept. For most of its farming practices it turns the clock back to 1950."
        —San Diego Center for Molecular Agriculture, a group of university and biotechnology scientists working in the San Diego, California area.

San Diego Center for Molecular Agriculture, "Foods from Genetically Modified Crops," San Diego, CA, undated.

Organic farmers also try to increase the number of beneficial soil organisms—both larger organisms such as earthworms and smaller ones such as microbial bacteria, algae, and fungi—all of which help to break down organic materials in the soil so that plants can use them as nutrients. Yet another common way of improving the fertility of the soil organically is by using what is called green manure. This involves planting one of several types of cover crops, such as clover, which pull nitrogen from the air. The cover crop is then plowed under, adding nitrogen to the soil as well as organic matter, which helps the soil to retain water and improves aeration. Finally, organic farmers rely heavily on crop rotation—that is, moving crops to different locations from year-to-year in order to prevent soil depletion.

Organic farmers control weeds and pests by natural methods, too. One method of weed control is called mulching, which involves covering the soil with a layer of natural material (such as sawdust or straw). Mulching also helps the soil retain water, prevents erosion, and keeps the soil warm, which helps seeds sprout. Often too, weeds are hand-picked, adding to the labor-intensive nature of organic farming. To control pests, organic farmers use many different techniques. Sometimes,

Potato plants are surrounded by mulch. Mulch is a layer of natural material that is used by organic farmers to control weeds, help the soil retain water, prevent erosion, and keep the soil warm.

insect and disease killing solutions made from plant extracts, called botanical pesticides, are used. Another commonly used natural pesticide is made from the bacterium Bacillus thuringiensis (Bt), which produces a toxin lethal to crop-eating caterpillars but harmless to people or vertebrate animals. Other natural pest control techniques include selecting pest-resistant varieties of crops, using mechanical insect traps, growing companion crops that help discourage pest infections, and encouraging predatory beneficial insects that eat other insects known to feed on cash crops.

A SPIRITUAL CHOICE

"The decision to attend to the health of one's habitat and food chain is a spiritual choice. It's also a political choice, a scientific one, a personal and a convivial [sociable] one."

—Barbara Kingsolver, best-selling American author
and organic food enthusiast.

Barbara Kingsolver, "A Good Farmer," *The Nation*, November 3, 2003, Vol. 277, Iss. 14, p. 11.

Crop diversity is also a typical characteristic of organic farming. Most organic farms plant a variety of crops rather than trying to specialize in just one or two. This variety simulates the biodiversity found in nature, is less stressful for the soil, supports a wider range of beneficial insects and soil microorganisms, and helps to ensure the overall fertility of the organic farm. Managing multiple crops, however, is often more labor-intensive than running a farm that focuses only on one or two main crops. Studies in the 1970s by Washington University, for example, found that about 11 percent more labor was required per unit of production for organic crops. As a result, many organic farms are small-scale operations, often less than 10 acres. Indeed, quite a few organic farms still specialize in growing fresh fruits and vegetables primarily for local restaurants and farmers' markets. Increasingly, however, some large organic farms are being created and run by major food corporations.

Organic farms that raise animals for meat, dairy products, and eggs typically try to provide humane living conditions similar to traditional farms of the past. At many of these farms, cattle and similar herd animals are given ample pastures to graze, and chickens have access to the outdoors where they can range freely. Crowded conditions that are characteristic of conventional livestock farms are usually avoided.

Certified "Organic" Labels

During the early days of organic farming—the 1950s, 1960s, and 1970s—there were no standards for organic produce. Eventually, some states began to formulate guidelines, leading to a patchwork of different standards. Today, however, there is one national legal standard for "organic" in the United States.

The U.S. government's regulations for organic food were developed by the Department of Agriculture (USDA) under the Or-

Organic Pet Food

Although it is still tiny compared to the overall U.S. pet food market, organic pet food sales are growing at nearly three times the rate of human organic food sales. Annual organic pet food sales totaled around $30 million in 2005, up from $14 million in 2003. Currently, however, there are no regulations governing organic pet food, although the U.S. Department of Agriculture (USDA) is reviewing standards that could go into effect in 2008. Organic pet food manufacturers, however, contend that their foods avoid chemical ingredients that could be harmful to pets—a goal attractive to many pet owners, many of whom consider their pets members of the family. The organic pet food industry is expected to benefit greatly from a March 2007 recall of more than 100 conventional brands of pet food manufactured by Canada's Menu Foods, Inc. The recall was announced after it was found that contaminated wheat gluten used in the pet foods caused kidney failure and/or death in hundreds of dogs and cats throughout the United States.

ganic Foods Production Act of 1990 (OFPA), and implemented in 2002. Generally speaking, the national organic standards are designed to preserve methods of farming that maintain fertile soils without the use of toxic fertilizers and pesticides, in order to avoid damage to the natural environment. This ecological purpose is included in the government's definition of "organic":

> Organic agriculture is an ecological production management system that promotes and enhances biodiversity, biological cycles and soil biological activity. It is based on minimal use of off-farm inputs and on management practices that restore, maintain and enhance ecological harmony. 'Organic' is a labeling term that denotes products produced under the authority of the Organic Foods Production Act. The principal guidelines for organic production are to use materials and practices that enhance the ecological balance of natural systems and that integrate the parts of the farming system into an ecological whole. Organic agriculture practices cannot ensure that products are completely free of residues; however, methods are used to minimize pollution from air, soil and water. Organic food handlers, processors and retailers adhere to standards that maintain the integrity of organic agricultural products. The primary goal of organic agriculture is to optimize the health and productivity of interdependent communities of soil life, plants, animals and people.[10]

In accordance with this definition, government regulations require "organic" food to be grown without most synthetic or chemical fertilizers and pesticides. Federal rules also require that fresh manure fertilizer must season, or be allowed to age, for 90 to 120 days after application before crops can be harvested (90 days if the harvested portion of the crop does not come in contact with the soil, 120 days if it does); this requirement helps to ensure that any dangerous pathogens (germs that cause diseases in humans) are destroyed and that food is safe for people to eat. In addition, the regulations prohibit the use of sewage sludge—

residues from treating human sewage—as a fertilizer, because it contains numerous heavy metals and other toxins. Similarly, organic products cannot be grown from genetically modified organisms (GMOs)—plants whose natural genetic make-up has been artificially altered by genetic engineering. Indeed, the USDA maintains a detailed list of approved and prohibited substances for organic farming.

However, the government's "organic" food label encompasses more than just fruit and vegetable crops; it also applies to grains, flowers, fiber crops (such as cotton, wool, and hemp), eggs and dairy, meat products, personal care products, and a variety of processed foods. For organic meat and poultry, the USDA rules prohibit the use of antibiotics or growth hormones. Nor can organic meat producers feed their animals food made from animal parts, because that practice has been shown to cause bovine spongiform encephalopathy (BSE), or mad cow disease—a chronic, degenerative nerve disorder affecting cattle

Animal feed made from animal parts. USDA regulations prevent organically raised cows from being fed food containing animal parts because it could contain bovine spongiform encephalopathy (BSE), or mad cow disease.

and sometimes people who consume their meat. Organically raised animals must also be given access to the outdoors. As for processed organic foods, they must be minimally processed without artificial ingredients or preservatives, and cannot be irradiated (a food safety technique that uses ionizing radiation to kill germs, but which has been criticized for depleting nutrients and posing health risks).

The regulations also require organic farmers to design and implement an "organic system plan" that describes the practices that will be used to produce organic crops and other products. The plan must specify how the farmer will manage the soil organically, what pest control methods will be used, what steps will be taken to create buffers to prevent contamination from neighboring non-organic farms, and the type of recordkeeping that will be employed to track products from the fields to the point of sale.

To ensure that these standards are met, national organic regulations require that organic growers and food handlers be certified by third-party state or private agencies or organizations that are accredited by USDA. Farmers and handlers who sell less than $5,000 a year in organic agricultural products are exempt from certification, but they still must meet all certified organic grower and handler requirements. USDA permits four types of organic labeling, depending on the percentage of organic content:

1. "100 percent Organic"—products that contain all organically produced ingredients may carry the USDA Organic Seal.

2. "Organic"—products made from at least 95 percent organic ingredients, and have remaining ingredients that are approved for use in organic production, may also carry the USDA Organic Seal.

3. "Made with Organic Ingredients"—products that contain at least 70 percent organic ingredients; up to three organic ingredients may be listed on the product's

The government imposes strict fines on companies that mislabel their products as "organic."

front packaging; but the product cannot carry the USDA Organic Seal.

4. Products with less than 70 percent organic ingredients, however, may only list the organic ingredients in small type in the ingredient listing on the product's side panel; no organic claims can be made on the front of the product packaging and the product cannot display the USDA Organic Seal.

These labels provide information for consumers so that they can trust that they are buying truly organic products.

Other Food Labels

Under current regulations, the penalty for knowingly selling or mislabeling as "organic" a product that was not produced and handled according to the government's organic rules is a fine of up to $10,000 per violation. Cases of blatant mislabeling have been rare so far. Sometimes, however, food producers use other labels to signify that their products are of a higher quality than conventionally grown foods, even if they do not meet the high standards for organic labels. These labels, however, are often confusing to consumers because they seem to suggest that foods meet organic or similar criteria.

ORGANIC VERSUS NON-ORGANIC

"No distinctions should be made between organically and non-organically produced products in terms of quality, appearance, or safety."

—U.S. Department of Agriculture, the federal
agency that regulates organic food.

Quoted in Stephen Barrett, "The Truth About Organic 'Certification:' Does It Help Ensure Safer Foods—Or Just Costlier Ones?," *Nutrition Forum*, March-April, 1998. http://findarticles.com/p/articles/mi_m0GCU/is_n2_v15/ai_20924353/pg_2.

One of the most commonly used labels, for example, is "natural." Although it suggests something close to "organic," the term "natural" is completely unregulated except for meat and poultry, and for those products, it does not affect how animals were raised. As environmental advocates David Joachim and Rochelle Davis explain:

> In truth, natural is an unregulated labeling term that refers to how a [meat] product is processed, not how it is produced. The U.S. Department of Agriculture (USDA) defines natural as simply 'a product containing no artificial ingredient or added color and is only minimally processed.[11]

Natural meats, therefore, can meet this definition, yet still be produced under conditions very similar to conventionally grown foods—for example, from confined animals who were given antibiotics, growth hormones, and non-organic animal feed.

A number of other labels confront consumers as well. Labels such as "hormone-free" and "antibiotic-free" (used in dairy products) or "free-range" (used for poultry), for example, help sell products but in reality are relatively vague and meaningless. Consumers are free to choose such products, but the government provides no certification or assurances that the producers' claims are, indeed, true. Only foods labeled "organic" are certified and meet USDA standards.

THE RISE OF THE ORGANIC FOOD MOVEMENT

T he seemingly new phenomenon of organic food is in some ways a return to the past. As many commentators have pointed out, all food was once produced naturally, until industrial farming techniques were developed in the late nineteenth and early twentieth centuries. At that point, most farmers in the United States began using synthetic chemical fertilizers and pesticides, mechanized farm equipment, and other modern farming practices, eventually changing the face of agriculture around the world. Fear that these chemicals and other industrial techniques could be affecting people's health and damaging the environment, in turn, has led consumers in recent decades to once again seek out food that is grown according to more natural farming methods. These naturally grown foods today are called organic.

Traditional Farming

Agriculture has existed for thousands of years, and for many generations most people in the world were directly connected to the land and the natural world. Most farms were owned by families who farmed the land to produce food for themselves and to trade for non-farm goods. Some larger farms rose above this subsistence level of agriculture and grew extra produce and raised animals for sale, to produce profits. In early America, for example, most people both lived and worked in rural environments doing farm-related tasks. As of 1800, in fact, approximately 75 percent of the population of the United States was directly engaged in agricultural production.

Early farming techniques by necessity were limited to natural methods for improving the soil, fertilizing plants, and minimizing pest and disease damage to crops. Although some early farmers were not as focused on building up the soil as today's organic farmers, traditional farming methods were all organic in the sense that they did not rely on synthetic chemicals, either for fertilizers or to discourage weeds and pests—because these chemicals did not exist. Early farmers also grew a variety of crops and raised a variety of farm animals, such as cattle, horses, goats, and chickens. Although animals were needed for basic transportation, hauling, and plowing, they also were raised for their meat, dairy products, and eggs, and they provided an abundant source of fertilizer with their manure. This variety of plants and animals and the recycling of wastes helped to make the traditional farm a sustaining, self-contained unit.

Pioneers using oxen to plow farmland. During the 1800s, approximately 75 percent of the American population was directly engaged in agriculture production.

The Rise of Industrial Farming

Farming methods underwent a sea change, however, beginning with the Industrial Revolution—a period in history beginning around the mid-1800s with the invention of new machines such as the steam engine, when many types of work became more mechanized. The invention of the internal combustion engine, powered by gasoline, in the late 1800s led to the replacement of animal labor with tractors, as well as to numerous other mechanized farm implements. Other developments changed farming as well, such as advances in plant breeding, the production of the first synthetic nitrogen fertilizers, and the invention of large-scale irrigation systems.

THE OLDEST FORM OF AGRICULTURE

"Organic farming is the oldest form of agriculture. Before the end of World War II, farming without the use of petroleum-based chemicals was the only option for farmers."

—Robin Brett Parnes, a public health expert and member of the editorial staff of the Maxwell & Eleanor Blum Patient and Family Learning Center at the Massachusetts General Hospital in Boston, Massachusetts.

Robin Brett Parnes, "How Organic Food Works," *How Stuff Works*, 2007. http://home.howstuffworks.com/organic-food8.htm#author.

These developments allowed farmers to more easily and efficiently till and plant much larger fields. Farms in the United States rapidly grew in size and began to specialize in just a few crops, in order to maximize farm profits. Family farms that could not compete in this new agriculture system were often bought up by larger farm corporations. Families that had farmed for many generations found themselves without land, their children moving into the cities to find factory jobs. As the Illinois State Museum explains:

A gradual change in approach and attitude towards our farmlands, the nation's heartland, took place. It reflected a change from a stewardship [caretaking] ethic, an agrar-

After World War II, it was common to see planes spraying the chemical DDT on crops in order to control pests.

ian [rural] philosophy, to one based on efficiency, commerce, and productivity.[12]

Following World War II, the nature of farming changed even more as American farmers increasingly relied on chemicals and technologies developed during the war to boost their farm production. Two chemicals developed during the war, in particular, were readily accepted for peacetime agricultural uses. One was ammonium nitrate, a chemical used in military weapons and ammunition, which became popular as a plant fertilizer because it was an abundant and cheap source of nitrogen. Another chemical, DDT, was a chemical pesticide that the military had used during the war to control disease-carrying insects; after the war, DDT was used widely in the United States to destroy agricultural pests. By the 1950s, family-run farms were fast disappearing and being replaced by massive, corporate-run agribusinesses dedicated to the marvels of modern, chemical- and machine-based farming.

The U.S. government supported the new farming advances and provided the growing agribusiness industry with help in the form of free technical advice, price guarantees on agriculture products, tax benefits, and large grants to encourage further technological development. Most agricultural research, both private and government sponsored, focused on industrial farming, and this brand of farming became the norm in the United States and other developed countries. The U.S. government also promoted industrial farming methods (such as hybrid plants, chemical fertilizers and pesticides, large-scale irrigation, and heavy mechanization) around the world as a way for developing countries to improve their agricultural output and profits.

The Roots of Organic Farming

Organic farming developed largely as a negative reaction to this new brand of industrial agriculture. A few farmers in the United States rejected the industrial/chemical approach, choosing instead to remain small in scale and use traditional farming methods, natural fertilizers, and non-toxic pest controls. Later, family farm crises brought by the wave of industrial agriculture, along with resulting declines in farm prices, also caused some conventional farmers to try organic farming as a way to attract higher prices for their crops, return to more satisfying farming practices, and save family farms. As organic advocate Deirdre Birmingham explains:

> Soils were losing their organic matter and inherent fertility. Streams were being polluted with soil and agricultural chemicals. The air was clouded with dust and increasingly befouled by the odors of animal farm-factories. Seeking a return to methods that worked with—and were good for—the natural environment, pioneering practitioners at first called their methods regenerative agriculture.[13]

These early organic farmers sold their organic produce wherever they could, often to local markets. Initially, people who bought organic produce tended to be local residents who knew the farmer personally and were looking for good quality and taste in their fruits and vegetables. In the 1960s and 1970s, however, books and news stories began to focus public awareness on pesticide dangers and other problems with conventional farming, helping to make organic foods popular among a wider group of consumers.

The most famous of these publications was a ground-breaking book, *Silent Spring*, published in 1962 by Rachel Carson, a former marine biologist with the U.S. Fish and Wildlife Service and a well-known author of books about nature. *Silent Spring* exposed the dangers of the then-widely-used pesticide DDT

Rachel Carson's groundbreaking book Silent Spring *brought to the public's attention the issue of just how dangerous chemical pesticides were to humas as well as to the environment.*

and other chemicals on the environment. Carson passionately argued that chemical poisons were slowly killing off the nation's birds and other creatures, which could one day produce a "silent spring" bereft of the sounds of chirping birds. As the environmental group Natural Resources Defense Council explains on their Web site:

> [Carson's book] described how DDT entered the food chain and accumulated in the fatty tissues of animals, including human beings, and caused cancer and genetic damage. A single application on a crop, she wrote, killed insects for weeks and months, and not only the targeted insects but countless more, and remained toxic in the environment even after it was diluted by rainwater. Carson concluded that DDT and other pesticides had irrevocably [permanently] harmed birds and animals and had contaminated the entire world food supply. The book's most haunting and famous chapter, "A Fable for Tomorrow," depicted a nameless American town where all life—from fish to birds to apple blossoms to human children—had been "silenced" by the insidious effects of DDT.[14]

Silent Spring became a bestseller in the United States and was read by many people around the world. It is credited with launching the environmental movement and with helping to convince the U.S. Congress to ban the use of DDT in 1972. As former Vice-President Al Gore wrote in an introduction to the 1994 edition of the book, "Without this book, the environmental movement might have been long delayed or never have developed at all."[15]

Even before the publication of *Silent Spring*, however, a few early visionaries had already begun promoting the benefits of organically farmed foods. One of these was Sir Albert Howard, a British botanist whom many consider to be the father of modern organic agriculture. Howard spent much of his career in India as an agricultural advisor, where he reportedly learned the connection between natural farming methods and human health. In 1943, he published *An Agricultural Testament*, a book that explained organic farming techniques, which he called "nature's farming," with an emphasis on the value of composting, or returning organic wastes back into farm soils. Howard's work influenced many organic farmers and scientists around the world.

One of Howard's admirers, an American named Jerome Irving Rodale, bought a farm in Emmaus, Pennsylvania, to try out organic farming techniques and soon dedicated himself to promoting organic farming throughout the United States. In 1930 Rodale founded a publishing house, the Rodale Press, and in 1942 he started the *Organic Farming and Gardening* magazine, with Albert Howard serving as associate editor. These businesses still exist today. Over the years, Rodale Press has published numerous books about organic farming and foods, and Rodale's gardening magazine claims to be the most widely read gardening publication in the world. In these publications, Rodale distributed information about organic farming and home gardening methods, promoted the health benefits of eating organic food, and helped greatly to popularize the term "organic" in the United States and other countries.

AN UNWINNABLE CHEMICAL WAR

"The chemical war is never won, and all life is caught in its violent crossfire."

—Rachel Carson, a former marine biologist with the U.S. Fish and Wildlife Service and a well-known author of books about nature and the environment.

Rachel Carson, *Silent Spring*, Boston, MA: Houghton Mifflin Co., 1962, p. 8.

Largely as a result of the efforts of Rachel Carson, Albert Howard, Jerome Irving Rodale and other pioneers, consumers began to search for foods that did not contain toxic chemicals. Many of these early organic consumers were young hippies who in the 1960s and 1970s identified with environmental causes. Some people during this period even started organic farms of

Pre-school children drinking apple juice amid the Alar scare in 1989. Many people believe that the Sixty Minutes *report on the dangers of Alar was the defining moment for the organic food industry.*

their own. Many commentators say, however, that the defining moment for organic food came in 1989, when the television show *Sixty Minutes* broadcast a story on Alar, a brand name for a chemical that farmers sprayed on apples to encourage entire crops to ripen at the same time. The show reported that Alar causes cancer, and that it is particularly dangerous for children. The apple industry disputed these claims, but overnight, the sales of apple products plummeted; Alar was pulled off the market; and the demand for organic food skyrocketed. This was the beginning of a small, niche market for early organic foods.

The Fight Over Organic Standards

As the market for organic foods grew, however, the need for uniform standards became increasingly clear because consumers needed to know which foods were truly produced organically. Jerome Irving Rodale helped to establish a set of voluntary standards and a certification program in 1972, and numerous states passed laws regulating organic agriculture beginning in the late 1970s. During this early period, the organic industry relied on state or accredited private agencies to evaluate organic farmers' practices to make sure they complied with state standards. Those farms that complied were permitted to market their products as "organic" and display an organic label on their packaging. These state laws produced a variety of somewhat conflicting standards, however; eventually, there were 44 different definitions of "organic" in the United States. By the 1980s farming and consumer groups were clamoring for a national, uniform standard.

The U.S. government's first foray into organic farming occurred in 1980, when the USDA, under the direction of Secretary of Agriculture Robert Bergland, investigated the organic farming industry and published the Report and Recommendations on Organic Farming—a report that recommended greater government support for organic agriculture and established an Office of Organic Resources Coordinator to aid in this effort. This support was short-lived, however, because in 1981 President Ronald Reagan's administration abolished the position of Organic Resources Coordinator and ended the USDA organic foods program. Government opposition toward organic agriculture during this early period was perhaps best illustrated by a comment attributed to former Secretary of Agriculture Earl Butz: "When you hear the word organic, think starvation."[15] Butz and other government leaders during the 1970s and 1980s remained committed to promoting the interests of large, corporate-owned agri-businesses, which focused solely on an industrial farming approach.

Public and organic industry pressure, however, ultimately persuaded Congress to pass the first organic food legislation—the Organic Foods Production Act (OFPA)—in 1990. The

OFPA established the National Organic Program (NOP) and created a National Organic Standards Board (NOSB) to develop a uniform set of standards for the United States organic market. The NOSB consisted of representatives from the following categories: farmer/grower; handler/processor; retailer; consumer/public interest; environmentalist; scientist; and certifying agent farmer/grower. Over the next five years, the NOSB held a series of public hearings and made its recommendations to the USDA in 1994.

THE DEBATE OVER ORGANIC IDEALS

"Tension and debate continues between the different philosophical, political and scientific ideas and ideals of organic and non-organic farming and even within the organic farming community itself."

—Joseph Heckman, a professor in the Plant Biology & Pathology Department at Rutgers University.

Joseph Heckman, "A History of Organic Farming—Transitions from Sir Albert Howard's War in the Soil to the USDA National Organic Program," *Wise Traditions in Food, Farming and the Healing Arts*, Winter 2006. www.westonaprice.org/farming/history-organic-farming.html#author.

The USDA considered the NOSB recommendations and issued its first set of organic regulations in 1997. These initial USDA regulations, however, were passionately and widely criticized by organic farmers and consumers for failing to incorporate the NOSB recommendations. Organic advocates, fearing that the federal government would weaken existing state organic standards, organized a broad-based opposition movement. Altogether, the USDA received a record number of 275,603 comments. Indeed, as Brian Baker of the Organic Materials Review Institute explains, "The USDA received more comments on the first proposed NOP Rule than any other proposed USDA rulemaking up to that date. Practically every comment opposed the USDA adoption of the 1997 proposal as the NOP Rule."[16]

The main criticisms contained in the comments concerned the use of three relatively new technologies: irradiation, genetically modified organisms (GMOs), and sewage sludge (also called

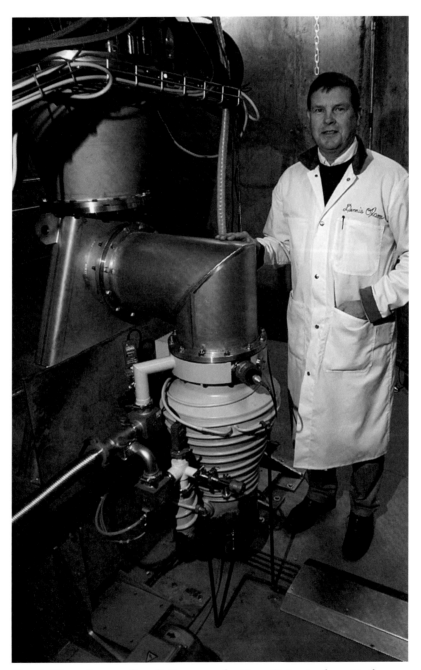

Dennis Olson, director of irradiation research at Iowa State, stands next to the linear accelerator used to zap meat with radiation. Opponents of irradiation believe that the process could be harmful to humans.

biosolid) fertilizers. These technologies had been approved by the government and were widely used in conventional farming, but organic advocates questioned their possible health effects and strenuously opposed their inclusion in organic foods. The objections to irradiation, for example, concerned whether the process reduces vitamin levels or creates high levels of free radicals that weaken cell membranes in a way that could be harmful to human health. In addition, critics argued that because irradiation does not kill all dangerous microbes, those that survive could mutate into even more deadly germs. Moreover, commentators said irradiation was simply a quick fix to hide the filthy conditions common in factory farming. Similarly, GMOs were seen by critics as possible "Frankenfoods"—artificial creations that could cause unforeseen, adverse health effects or spread throughout the natural environment killing native plants and creating genetic pollution. Critics also worried that GMOs would allow corporations to essentially establish patents on nature. And although it seems like an environmentally sound idea to recycle sewage sludge into agricultural fertilizer, the complaints pointed out that much of the sludge contains not just organic wastes, but also heavy metals, dangerous viruses, dioxins, PCBs, pesticides and hundreds of other toxic chemicals.

Ultimately, the USDA listened to the criticisms and incorporated most of the NOSB's recommendations into final regulations that were published on December 21, 2000, and implemented in final form on October 22, 2002. The final regulations are very lengthy but in general they prohibit the use of most synthetic fertilizers, pesticides, and other chemicals on crops as they grow and on the land during the last three years. Irradiation, GMOs, and sewage sludge technologies are also prohibited, along with the use of antibiotics and hormones, and organic foods must be protected from contamination from non-organic foods. "Prohibited" and "allowed" substances are carefully defined in a National List of Allowed and Prohibited Substances. After a tumultuous beginning, the USDA ultimately adopted relatively strong organic standards.

A Booming Organic Industry

The development of standards for organic production gave stability to the organic market and helped the already healthy organic food market to grow by leaps and bounds in recent years. Indeed, organic products are now the fastest growing segment of the U.S. agriculture market. As agricultural lawyer David K. Bowles puts it, "The market for organic foods has rapidly expanded from a fringe element of the agriculture industry to a healthy market."[17] Bowles explains that in 1980, U.S. sales of organic foods totaled only about $170 million, but by 1996 it had expanded to $3.5 billion—a twenty-fold increase in just sixteen years. The years since the finalization of federal standards have seen more remarkable growth. In 2005, for example, the Organic Trade Association reported that organic foods grew 16.2 percent and accounted for $13.8 billion in retail sales.

Organic Leaders—Whole Foods and Wild Oats

The two biggest names in the natural and organic food industry are Whole Foods and Wild Oats. Whole Foods began as a small company that catered to hippies wanting nutritious, vegetarian foods, but over the years it has experienced tremendous growth. By 2006, it operated numerous large, supermarket-style stores, each of them offering a full range of natural and organic foods, complete with upscale attractions such as delis, meat and fresh seafood offerings, and extensive wine selections. In fact, Whole Foods has earned the nickname, "Whole Paycheck," because many of its products tend be quite expensive. Wild Oats carries the same type of natural and organic products as Whole Foods, but it is much smaller in size, often offers lower prices, and is not nearly as profitable as its larger rival. In February 2007, Whole Foods announced it plans to purchase Wild Oats. The merger was challenged by the U.S. Federal Trade Commission (FTC), but if permitted, it will help provide Whole Foods with more locations and allow it to expand quickly, enabling it to better compete with mainstream grocers such as Safeway and Wal-Mart that are moving into the organic market.

Whole Foods Market is a supermarket-like store that carries a wide-range of organic foods, beverages, and wines. Although the company offers an extensive selelction, its prices tend to be quite expensive.

Nonfood organic products, such as clothing, flowers, pet foods, household cleaners, and personal care products, accounted for another $744 million in sales in 2005, creating a total 2005 organic sales record of about $15 billion. Sales of organic products are expected to continue this strong growth, so sales numbers will likely rise even higher in coming decades.

Fresh produce is still the top-selling organic food product, and organic dairy products are also very popular, but the fastest-growing organic food category is organic meat, which grew more than 50 percent in 2005. Organic flowers, pet food, and fibers are the categories of nonfood organic products most in demand. And hundreds of new organic products are introduced each year.

Since the early 1990s, the number of acres of organic farmland has also increased along with consumer demand. According to the USDA, certified organic farmland doubled between 1992 and 1997, and has continued to increase since then. Organic farms can now be found in all fifty states and account for more than 4 million acres of farmland, about 2.3 million acres for crops and 1.7 million acres for pasture- and rangeland for animals. California is the leading producer of organic items, with more than 220,000 acres dedicated to organic farms, mostly for fruit and vegetable production. Other top states for certified organic cropland include North Dakota, Montana, Minnesota, Wisconsin, Texas, and Idaho. Four states—Alaska, Texas, California and Montana—each have more than 100,000 acres of organic pasture- and rangeland.

The dramatic growth in the organic industry, in turn, has led the federal government to provide more funding for organic farming research and other programs. The lead government agency for many of these research programs is the USDA's Sustainable Agriculture and Education (SARE) program. Many of the government-funded studies have involved various aspects of organic agriculture, everything from soil and natural resource management and other facets of organic farming to the nutritional value of organic foods. Other research has focused on the economics of organic farming—its yields, input

An Organic Success Story

Earthbound Farms is one of the best success stories in the organic foods market. The company, located in California, was started 22 years ago by two New Yorkers, Myra and Drew Goodman, who sold raspberries and baby greens from their home garden to a local restaurant. When a new chef didn't want their greens, the two entrepreneurs put them into bags and sold them. Today, bagged salad greens can be found in most American supermarkets, as well as in organic and natural food stores, and Earthbound Farms is now the biggest organic produce company in the United States, reporting $450 million in sales in 2006. Earthbound today farms 26,000 organic acres in five Western states, British Columbia, Mexico, New Zealand, and Chile. In fact, the company ships its products such great distances that some organic advocates criticize it for adopting industrial farming methods. Earthbound owners, however, defend their environmental record, pointing out that they keep 4,200 tons of chemical fertilizers and 135 tons of pesticides out of the environment every year. Earthbound spinach was implicated in a recent e.coli outbreak, but the company's growth is expected to continue along with the rest of the organic market.

costs, income, profitability, and other economic factors. Studies also have been done on consumer motivations for buying organic. Consumers cited health, environment, and taste as the top three reasons for their organic preferences, and the main predictor of whether people buy organic appears to be price and people's income levels.

Despite this growing organic market, however, in the United States organic farms still make up only about 2 percent of all farming operations. Most organic farms remain small, most less than 100 acres. Nevertheless, more uniform standards and the booming demand for organic foods are encouraging larger producers to enter the field of organic food production. This development is rapidly changing the organic industry from one dominated by small farmers who mainly grew fresh fruits and vegetables to one in which a wide variety of organic products are produced, sometimes by very large farms owned by corporations.

Organic advocates hope this increasing focus by government and corporate interests on the organic industry signals a widespread return to more natural farming methods like those employed before the advent of industrial farming. The new interest in organic products could even improve organic farming techniques and make today's organic farms much more sustainable and profitable than traditional farms of the pre-industrial era. Supporters say these developments, if they occur, would be good for both health and the environment.

Myra and Drew Goodman cofounded Earthbound Farms in the 1980s and it is now the largest organic produce company in the United States.

ARE THERE HEALTH BENEFITS TO EATING ORGANIC FOOD?

Consumers are repeatedly assured that conventionally grown food is safe, nutritious, and abundant. Organic advocates, however, claim that food grown or produced by industrial, chemical-based farming methods is dangerous to human health, possibly even a contributing cause of many cases of cancer. Those who buy organic products often do so because they believe that organic foods grown without using synthetic chemical fertilizers and pesticides are more nutritious and healthier than non-organic foods. So far, however, there is no conclusive scientific proof of this claim, and conventional farming supporters say that organic food, in some ways, may pose more dangers than conventionally grown food.

The Problems with Industrial Food

Industrial agriculture companies spend billions to portray their foods as healthy, nutritious, and safe. Modern supermarkets are filled with colorful, attractively packaged products and perfect-looking fruit and vegetables, and large industrial agricultural companies proclaim their commitment to health and the environment. The company Web site for Monsanto, a seller of agricultural chemicals and also a producer of GMO foods, for example, claims the company is helping farmers to "produce healthier foods,...while also reducing agriculture's impact on our environment."[18] The U.S. government generally reinforces these positive food messages. Representatives from the USDA and the

U.S. Food and Drug Administration (FDA), for example, repeatedly assure the American public that the U.S. food supply is the safest in the world.

Critics of industrial foods and organic advocates, however, paint a much more foreboding picture of industrial food. They argue that many of the fertilizers used by conventional farm operations contain toxins and heavy metals known to be harmful to humans. Organic advocates also point out that the factory farming of animals helps to spread disease and has led to a rise in food-borne illnesses in the United States in recent years. Meanwhile, consumer groups argue that milk from cows treated with growth hormones contributes to increased cancer risk. In addition, the widespread use of antibiotics in animal production is viewed by many as the main reason that antibiotics are losing their effectiveness against infectious bacteria.

Another concern is that conventional farms give cows animal feed made from parts of dead cows, some of which may have had bovine spongiform encephalopathy (BSE) or mad cow disease, a fatal brain-wasting disease. This practice has been shown to spread BSE through cattle herds. Persons who eat beef contaminated with BSE can, in turn,

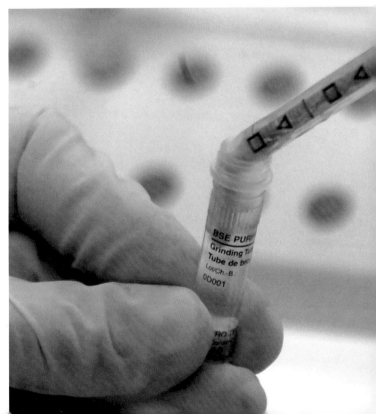

Brain parts, extracted from cow heads, are being prepared for a special BSE, or mad cow disease test. Conventional farming may spread mad cow disease through a heard of cows by feeding the cows contaminated feed.

Type	Examples	Characterisitcs
Insecticides		
Inorganic chemicals	Mercury, lead, arsenic, copper sulfate	Highly toxic to many organisms, persistent, bio accumulates
Organochlorines	DDT, methoxychlor, heptachlor, HCH pentachloraphenol, chlordanc, toxaphene, aldrin, endrin, dieldrin, lindane	Mostly neurotoxinxs, cheap, persistent, fast acting, easy to apply, broad spectrum, bioaccumulates, biomagnifies
Organophosphates	Parathion, melathion, diazinion, dichlorves, phosdrin, disulforon, TEPP, DDVP	More soluble, extremely toxic nerve poisions, fast acting, quickly degrade, toxic to many organisms. Very dangerous to farm workers
Carbamates and Urethanes	Carbaryl (Sevin), aldicarb, carbofuran, methomyl, Temik mancozeb	Quickly degraded, do not bioaccumulate, toxic to broad spectrum of organisms, fast acting, very toxic to honey bees
Formamoidines	Amitraz, chlordimeform (Fundal and Galecron)	Neurotoxins specific for certain stages of insect development, act synergistically with other insecticides
Microbes	*Bacillus thuringensis*	Kills caterpillars
	Bacillus popilliae Viral diseases	Kills beetles Attack a variety of moths and caterpillars
Plant products and synthetic analogs	Nicotine, rotenone, pyethrum,alletbrin, docamethrin, resmethrin, fenralcrate, permethrin, tetramethrin	Natural botanical products and synthetic analogs, fast acting, broad insecticide action, low toxicity to mammals, expensive
Fungicides	Captan, manch, zench, dinocap, folpet, pentachlorphenol, menthyl bromide, carbon bisulfide, chlorothaionil (Bravo)	Most prevent fungal spore germination and stop plant diseases: among most widley used pesticides in United States.
Fumigants	Ethylene dibromide, dibronochloropropane, carbon tetrachloride, carbon disulfide, methyl bromide	Used to kill nomatodes, fungi insects, and other pests in soil, grain, fruits; highly toxic, cause neve damage, sterility, cancer, birth defects
Herbicides	2,4 D: 2,4,5T, paraquat, dinoseb, Silvex, linuron	Block photosyntyhesis, act as hormones to disrupt plant growth and development, or kill soil microorganisms essential for plant growth

This table lists different pesticides and their characteristics. Scientists have found that most pesticides can be classified as carcinogenics.

contract the human version of mad cow disease, Creutzfeldt-Jacob disease.

The main criticism of industrial food, however, is directed at synthetic pesticide use. Critics say chemical pesticides are poisons developed to kill hardy insects and weeds, so they believe it is likely these chemicals are dangerous to humans. In fact studies have linked many of the pesticides used in conventional farming with cancer and other diseases. Ingestion of these chemicals over a lifetime, critics say, is dangerous to human health.

The Danger of Synthetic Pesticides

Critics of industrial food cite certain government research studies to support their claim of chemical pesticide dangers. A 1987 report by the National Academy of Sciences (NAS), an institution of distinguished scientists created to provide advice to the federal government, estimated that 60 percent of all herbicides, 90 percent of all fungicides, and 30 percent of all insecticides used on U.S. crops at that time consisted of materials the U.S. Environmental Protection Agency (EPA) classified as carcinogenic. And in 1998, Dr. Lynn Goldman of the EPA confirmed that at least 101 pesticides used in the United States are probable or possible human carcinogens. Critics are also concerned about what unforeseen harm combinations of different toxins might cause.

DEADLY INDUSTRIAL FOOD

"Contrary to our government's pronouncement, industrial food is not safe. It is, in fact, becoming increasingly deadly and devoid of nutrition."

—Andrew Kimbrell, a public interest attorney, activist, author, and director of the Center for Food Safety, a public interest and environmental advocacy membership organization.

Andrew Kimbrell, "Seven Deadly Myths of Industrial Agriculture," *Fatal Harvest: The Tragedy of Industrial Agriculture*, Andrew Kimbrell, ed., Washington, D.C.: Island Press, 2002, p. 53.

The 12 Fruits and Vegetables with the Most Pesticide Residues

According to the Environmental Working Group (EWG), an environmental research group, the twelve most pesticide-laden fruits and vegetables (in order of toxicity) are:

1. Strawberries
2. Bell Peppers
3. Spinach
4. Cherries (from the United States)
5. Peaches
6. Cantaloupe (from Mexico)
7. Celery
8. Apples
9. Apricots
10. Green Beans
11. Grapes (from Chile)
12. Cucumbers

Other produce items, however, tend to have low amounts of pesticide residues. There's almost no benefit to buying organic bananas, for example, because any pesticide residue is probably thrown out, along with the peel. Other foods low in pesticides include broccoli, sweet potatoes, brussels sprouts, cabbage, onions, asparagus, and blueberries.

Most of these potentially carcinogenic pesticides are still legally used in industrial farming today. Many of these legal pesticides were approved by the EPA years ago, before research linked them with cancer and other diseases. And although Congress in the 1996 Food Quality Protection Act (FQPA) required the EPA to reassess the safety of all U.S. pesticides, the agency has come under criticism for failing to err on the side of safety in its decisions. In fact, only a relatively few pesticides have been banned or significantly restricted by the EPA in this process, and critics, including some of the EPA's own scientists, claim the agency also approved many pesticides that may be toxic to humans.

Illegal pesticides may present additional dangers. Studies by the FDA and private groups have found that a percentage of conventionally grown foods contain either pesticides that are il-legal for that particular food crop or pesticide levels that exceed government limits. The research organization Environmental Working Group (EWG), for example, analyzed 14,923 records of FDA pesticide-monitoring data on 42 fruits and vegetables for the years 1992 and 1993. They found that 5.6 percent of this produce contained pesticides or pesticide levels that violated government standards. Certain items (green peas, pears, apple juice, blackberries, green onions, hot peppers, green beans, strawberries, and carrots) had much higher violation rates. Ad-ditionally, in four common foods (bulb onions, apple juice, green peas, and green onions) between one-third and one-half of the pesticides detected were illegal. The EWG concluded that "illegal pesticides are pervasive and systemic across the fruit and vegetable industry."[19]

These pesticides, whether legal or illegal, leave chemical residues on fruits and vegetables that often cannot be easily washed off or removed before eating. Studies show these pesti-cides accumulate in people's bodies over time. A 2003 study of 9,282 Americans by the U.S. Center for Disease Control (CDC) found that over half of the people tested had at least eighteen of the twenty-three pesticides evaluated in their systems, and the average person tested positive for thirteen pesticides. Fur-ther, almost all the persons tested had two of the most danger-ous pesticides in their systems—TCP (found in 93 percent) and DDE, a breakdown product of DDT (found in 99 percent). In many cases, the pesticide levels in people's bodies far exceeded the levels established by the government as safe. Two pesticides in particular—chlorpyrithos and methyl parathion—exceeded "acceptable" government levels dramatically. Indeed, levels of chlorpyrithos, an insecticide sold by Dow Chemical Company under the brand name Dursban, averaged about 3 to 4.6 times what government agencies consider safe for chronic exposure.

It is difficult, however, to prove a clear scientific connection between specific diseases and widespread environmental fac-tors. There are ethical problems with running tests on humans that would purposely expose them to potentially dangerous

Shown here are two "normal" frogs and four frogs with deformities. A study conducted on the frogs found that the deformities were caused due to the frogs exposure to pesticides.

chemicals, so studies are usually performed on animals. However, these animal studies, as well as studies of farming populations that work with pesticides suggest that pesticide exposure may play a role in causing a variety of diseases and conditions. As scientist and internationally known conservationist Jane Goodall explains:

> One of the greatest controversies surrounding ... farm chemicals is how much exposure is considered safe for

humans. There is still a great deal more research that needs to be done, but we certainly know, for sure, that exposure to chemical pesticides is linked to various forms of cancer, as well as Parkinson's disease, miscarriages, and birth defects.[20]

The exact nature of the link, how much exposure is dangerous to humans, and even how much of the pesticide residue is transferred from produce to people, is still a matter of some controversy.

The Most Vulnerable Populations

Many scientists believe that pesticides are particularly damaging for fetuses, infants, and young children. A 1993 report by NAS supported these concerns, finding that children have higher

Effects of Organic Foods on Children

Organic advocates urge consumers to purchase organic foods for their children to protect them from the toxins in pesticides, and recent studies suggest that making the switch to organic can have dramatic and immediate results. A study funded by the U.S. Environmental Protection Agency (EPA) and reported in 2005, for example, found that many pesticides in children's urine decrease to nondetectable levels as soon as they began eating organic foods. In the study, scientists from the University of Washington, Emory University, and the Centers for Disease Control and Prevention analyzed urine samples from twenty-three children in the Seattle area, ages three to eleven, for fifteen days. For the first three and the last seven days, the children ate their normal diets, but during the middle five days, they were fed only organic foods. Researcher discovered that residues of two common pesticides, malathion and chlorpyrifos, dropped immediately as soon as they switched to organic foods, but quickly climbed as soon as they resumed their conventional diets. Organic supporters point to the study as proof of the benefits of organics for young children, but supporters of conventional food maintain that there is no reason to switch to an organic diet since there is no clear scientific evidence that low levels of pesticides in foods cause serious harm.

metabolic rates and other unique body processes that can elevate the toxicity of various pesticides. In fact, NAS concluded that carcinogenic pesticides may be up to 10 times more toxic to infants and children than adults. More recently, the anti-pesticide group Pesticide Action Network, using CDC data, found that young children under six years of age carry significantly higher levels of pesticides than either adults or older children. Experts fear that these pesticides may be a major contributor to today's rising cancer epidemic among American children—an epidemic that now accounts for almost 10 percent of all childhood deaths. In addition, studies by the National Cancer Institute and others have shown a link between children's risk of leukemia and other cancers with exposure to pesticides.

LOW RISKS FROM PESTICIDES

"The risk from pesticide residue [in food], if any, is minuscule, is not worth worrying about, and does not warrant paying higher prices."
—Manfred Kroger, a professor of Food Science at Pennsylvania State University.

Quoted in Stephen Barrett, "Organic" Foods: Certification Does Not Protect Consumers," *Quackwatch*, July 17, 2006. www.quackwatch.org/01QuackeryRelatedTopics/organic.html.

Some of the most dangerous of the legal pesticides for children, according to experts, are organophosphates, a type of chemical toxin that can cause long-term damage to the brain and the nervous system and that is present in many of the pesticides used by today's farmers. A study by the Environmental Working Group (EWG) in 1998 found that infants and children are most at risk from consuming these pesticides, because their small, rapidly growing bodies are especially vulnerable to nerve damage during fetal development, infancy, and early childhood. The EPA has now banned or substantially reduced the use of two of the most dangerous of these chemicals—methyl parathion and azinphos-methyl—but at least thirty-eight other organophosphate pesticides remain on the market.

Although this farm worker is wearing protective gear, those farm workers who are exposed to pesticides on a regular basis and do not wear the appropriate protection are at the greatest risk for health problems.

Health risks from pesticides, however, might be the greatest for farmers and farm workers who are directly exposed to industrial pesticides when they are sprayed onto crops or when crops are picked. CDC data confirms that Mexican-Americans, who often are employed as farm workers, show much higher levels of pesticides in their bodies than other ethnic groups. A 1993 study by the National Cancer Institute found that farming communities tend to have significantly higher rates of a variety of cancers—including leukemia, non-Hodgkin's lymphoma, multiple myeloma, soft tissue sarcomas, and cancers of the skin, lip, stomach, brain, and prostate. Because of these types of study results, researchers suspect pesticides may be a significant factor in a number of types of cancer. Not surprisingly, the United Farm Workers, a union founded by labor organizer César Chávez to represent farm workers in the United States, has long fought for worker protections against pesticides.

Continuing Pesticide Dangers

Pesticides applied to crops over many decades, including very toxic ones that have since been banned by the U.S. government, have also slowly leaked into ground water used for drinking, adding to their potential health threat. According to the Environmental Working Group (EWG), for example, tap water in California's Central Valley, a prime agricultural area, contains extremely high, unsafe concentrations of DBCP, a now-banned pesticide considered to be one of the most potent pesticide carcinogens. The EPA confirms that more than 635 miles of rivers and streams in the Central Valley are so polluted by agricultural pesticides that they are unsafe for drinking, fishing, or even swimming.

Despite the suspected dangers, however, pesticide use in conventional farm operations has increased year after year. More and more chemicals have to be used because pests adapt over time, decreasing the pesticides' effectiveness. As Jane Goodall explains:

> After more than fifty years of farming with pesticides, there are whole populations of 'pest' insects that have evolved to become increasingly impervious to pesticides. The response of the farmer is to spray more often, and with increasingly more toxic pesticides. Nowadays, it's not uncommon for farmers to use three times as many chemicals as they needed forty years ago to kill off the same insects.[21]

Experts say since 1989, total pesticide use in the United States has grown by at least 8 percent, or 60 million pounds.

The Health Benefits of Organic Food

To protect themselves from pesticide dangers, many people avoid conventionally grown foods and buy only organic produce and food products. Although no food will ever be completely free of pesticides due to the wide dispersal of pesticides in our environment, current organic standards ensure that foods that are labeled organic have met criteria aimed at minimizing synthetic fertilizers and pesticides. Because of children's susceptibility to toxins, organic advocates believe organic foods may be most beneficial for children and pregnant women.

Recent studies show that organic foods are much less likely to contain pesticide residues. A major study by scientists from the Organic Materials Review Institute (OMRI), an independent organic agriculture research organization, and the consumer group Consumers Union (CU), for example, was completed in 2002. The study, which analyzed more than 94,000 food samples of about 20 different crops over nearly a decade, found that about 73 percent of conventionally grown produce had pesticide residues (especially certain crops, such as apples, peaches, pears, strawberries, and celery), often from multiple pesticides. By comparison, only about 23 percent of organically grown samples of the same crops contained any level of pesticides. Brian Baker, OMRI's research director, concluded, "Our research con-

Studies have shown that conventionally farmed produce, like apples, are more likely to contain pesticide residue.

firms what organic farmers have known all along, but now we have the data to back it up....Organic food clearly offers consumers the best choice to avoid pesticides in their diets."[22]

Organic advocates also say that organic foods taste better and are more nutritious. A study published by trace minerals analyst Bob L. Smith in the *Journal of Applied Nutrition* in 1993, for example, compared organically and conventionally grown apples, potatoes, pears, wheat and sweet corn were purchased over a two-year period in the Chicago suburbs. Researchers found that the organically grown food was on average 63 percent higher in calcium, 73 percent higher in iron, 118 percent higher in magnesium, 178 percent higher in molybdenum, 91 percent higher in phosphorus, 125 percent higher in potassium, and 60 percent higher in zinc. Similar results were found in a 2001 review by nutritionist Virginia Worthington of forty-one studies comparing the nutritional value of organic and conventional produce. Worthington concluded that organic produce had on average 27 percent more vitamin C, 21.1 percent more iron, 29.3 percent more magnesium, and 13.6 percent more phosphorous than conventional produce.

DANGERS FROM ORGANIC FOOD

"Despite the claims of organic farmers and their supporters, organic food is more dangerous than produce grown by conventional farming methods."

—Dennis T. Avery, director of the Center for Global Food Issues, an agricultural and environmental research project of the conservative think-tank, the Hudson Institute.

Dennis T. Avery, "The Hidden Dangers in Organic Food," *American Outlook*, Fall 1998.

Meanwhile, scientists from the University of California, Davis, in a 2003 article published in the *Journal of Agricultural and Food Chemistry*, found that organically grown foods tend to be significantly higher in cancer-fighting antioxidants than conventionally grown foods. The study examined several crops for their levels of flavonoids, defensive antioxidants produced by plants to combat environmental stresses, such as insects or competing plants. The study found that the levels of antioxidants in organically grown corn and marionberries (a type of blackberry) were 50 percent higher than their conventionally grown counterparts, and for organic strawberries levels were 19 percent higher. The research suggested that chemical pesticides reduced the need for plants to produce these defensive chemicals.

Organic advocates say that the best organic choices are foods that are grown locally. Foods that must be shipped to distant locations are often picked before they are ripe, to allow for between one and two weeks of shipping and selling time. Produce destined to be sold locally, on the other hand, can be picked and sold often within 24 hours, at the height of ripeness, when it has the best flavor and the greatest amount of nutrients.

Defending Industrial Food

Despite these findings, however, supporters of conventionally grown foods maintain that there is no clear scientific evidence

The USDA Organic label certifies which foods have met the USDA standards for products grown without synthetic pesticides or other chemicals. It does not insinuate that the product is in any way safer thean other food products.

that organic food is healthier than conventional foods. Even the world-renowned medical facility, the Mayo Clinic, advises, "No conclusive evidence shows that organic food is more nutritious than conventionally grown food ... [In addition,] most experts agree...that the amount of pesticides found on fruits and vegetables poses a very small health risk."[23] Notably, too, both organic and conventional foods must pass the same government safety standards, and the U.S. government makes no claim that organic foods are in any way safer or more healthy. The USDA organic regulations merely define what foods may carry an organic label; they do not address food safety or nutrition. As former Agriculture Secretary Dan Glickman has pointed out, "The organic label is a marketing tool. It is not a statement about food safety."[24]

THE FAILURE TO PROTECT PUBLIC HEALTH

"The fact that we all carry a mix of toxic pesticides in our bodies represents a dramatic failure of government efforts to protect public health and safety. Rather than focusing on preventing harm, current pesticide policies are designed to weigh health and environmental concerns against the economic interests of pesticide manufacturers, users and their allies."

—Kristen S. Schafer, Margaret Reeves, Skip Spitzer, and Susan E. Kegley, researchers at Pesticide Action Network (PAN) North America, a public interest organization that works to replace chemical pesticides with ecologically sound alternatives.

Kristen S. Schafer, Margaret Reeves, Skip Spitzer, and Susan E. Kegley, "Chemical Trespass: Pesticides in Our Bodies and Corporate Responsibility: Executive Summary," *Pesticide Action Network North America*, May 2004.

Defenders of industrial food reject the cited studies that purport to show a link between pesticides and cancer, or that suggest greater nutrition levels or lower levels of pesticides in organic foods. Government studies, they say, contradict the findings of many consumer groups and show that most conventionally grown foods contain little or no pesticides by the time they reach consumers. A 2002 FDA study of both U.S. and imported food, for example, found no pesticide residues in 71.9 percent of the U.S. samples and in 83.1 percent of the imported samples. Moreover, only 15 percent of conventionally raised meat tested by the USDA in 2002 was found to contain any detectible pesticide residues. And those foods that do test positive for pesticides, defenders argue, usually contain only very tiny, trace amounts that have not been proven to cause any health effects in humans.

In fact, critics claim that studies of pesticides are often based on lab tests in which small animals such as mice are fed very large quantities of pesticides—a far cry from the minute residues left on fruits and vegetables and consumed by humans. Tests are done on animals because of the ethical problems involved with subjecting human test subjects to substances that could cause cancer. In deciding what levels of pesticides are safe, the EPA then assumes that adult humans may be 10 fold more sensitive than animals, and that children may be 100-fold more sensitive. Reporter Rob Lyons concludes, "There is no evidence of anybody ever dying or falling seriously ill from eating food carrying traces of man-made pesticides."[25]

As for studies that conclude that organic food is more nutritious, industrial food supporters argue that the overall evidence is weak. A 2004 review of the existing research on this issue by Ruth Kava of the American Council on Science and Health, for example, concluded that neither organic nor conventional foods have consistently been shown to be superior in nutrient content. Although some studies show organic foods contain more nutrients, other studies confirm that organic and conventional foods are equally nutritious. A study published in 2006 by German scientists, for example, found that organically grown wheat contains essentially the same amino acids, sugars, and other substances as wheat grown by conventional farming methods.

Many researchers believe that nutrition levels actually vary widely in both organic and conventional foods, depending on the crop type, soil content, growing conditions, degree of freshness, cooking/shipping/processing methods, and other factors. A tomato grown by conventional methods, therefore, may be just as likely to have the same nutrients as an organically grown tomato. As David Miliband, Secretary of Britain's Department for Environment, Food, and Rural Affairs (DEFRA), stated in early 2007, "There isn't any evidence either way that's conclusive [about the health benefits of organic food]."[26] Critics point out that even the famous organic advocate J.I. Rodale failed to realize health benefits from organic food: On June 7, 1971, Rodale promised to live to be 100 thanks to his organic diet, but the next day, he died of a heart attack at age 73.

Toxins in Organic Farming

Defenders of industrial farming methods also claim that organic farming employs as many or sometimes even more toxins than conventionally grown foods. First, critics note that organic food is not pesticide-free. Chemical pesticides are now part of the natural environment, so they can drift in the air onto organic fields or be found in the water used for organic irrigation.

Critics of organic food also argue that the risks of food-borne illnesses, such as salmonella and E. coli, are greater with organically produced foods because raw animal manure is commonly used as fertilizer. This manure, critics say, can carry

A truck spreads manure on an organic lettuce farm. Critics claim that the use of organic materials, such as manure, increases the risks of foodborne illnesses like salmonella and E. coli.

various pathogens, including a new, dangerous strain of salmonella, S. typhimurium, as well as E. coli O157:H7, a type of toxic bacteria that can cause permanent liver and kidney damage and even death. In fact, critics say, the U.S. Centers for Disease Control (CDC) have reportedly linked a disproportionately large number of confirmed E. coli 0157 cases to organic foods. One well-known case occurred in 1996, when more than seventy people were sickened and one young girl died from E. coli 0157 as a result of drinking unpasteurized apple juice produced by the Odwalla Juice Company, an organic producer. More recently, in September 2006, an outbreak of E. coli 0157 on spinach was eventually traced to Natural Selection Foods, a California organic food company that supplies produce to large organic brands such as Earthbound Farm. Based on the CDC data, Dennis T. Avery, Director of the Center for Global Food Issues, claims that "people who eat organic and 'natural' foods are eight times as likely as the rest of the population to be attacked by...E. coli bacteria."[27]

Organic critics reject organic farmers' claims that they season manure until it is safe. A study at the University of California at Davis, for example, found that E. coli 0157 bacteria can only be killed if it is composted for a long period in intensive 160-degree temperatures. Typical organic composting typically only reaches about 130 degrees, critics say, and most organic farmers do not use thermometers to check the temperatures of their compost piles to ensure that all dangerous bacteria are destroyed.

Another potential problem is that organic food may be more likely to develop molds that contain mycotoxins, or fungal poisons. This is because organic crops are more often attacked by rodents and other pests, creating openings for fungal infections, and fungicides are not allowed in the production and processing of organic foods. As a result, critics say, organic crops tend to have higher rates of infestation by fungal toxins, including aflatoxin, a dangerous carcinogen. Whether organic foods are safer and healthier than conventional foods, therefore, is still very much a subject of scientific and public debate.

ORGANIC FARMING, THE ENVIRONMENT, AND SOCIETY

Organic food supporters not only claim that organic farming produces healthier food; they also say it is good for the environment and society. By avoiding synthetic fertilizers and pesticides, advocates say, organic farms contribute less pollution into the soil, ground waters, and the surrounding environment than chemical-based farming methods. In addition, the methods used by organic farms focus on building up the soil in ways that promote environmental biodiversity and sustainability. Critics of organic food, however, point out that these benefits come at a cost to consumers, and they argue that some organic products can be more harmful to the natural environment than industrially produced items.

The Environmental Costs of Conventional Farming

Organic advocates warn that conventional farming practices are poisoning the natural environment. Many scientists agree that decades of using synthetic fertilizer and pesticides, combined with other conventional farm practices that damage and erode the soil, is damaging the environment not only in the United States, but around the world.

Soil degradation is cited as one of the most pressing environmental problems caused by conventional agriculture. Growing one or two crops year after year in the same soil, many scientists say, depletes the soil of important nutrients, and the application of chemical fertilizers poses additional soil problems. Nearly all crops grown by industrial agriculture methods, for example, are given more nitrogen than they can use, and this overload of one nutrient can cause soil imbalances that create dead zones where plants cannot grow. The UN Food and Agriculture Organization (FAO) also says substantial soil damage is caused by using large tractors and ploughs—a practice long employed by big industrial agricultural companies. This intensive machine tillage tends to stir up the soil, allowing it to more easily be blown away as dust or eroded by rain and water run-off. Indeed, according to the international food research group, the International Food Policy Research Institute (IFPRI), almost 40 percent of the world's agricultural land is now seriously damaged, with the worst damage in developing regions such as Central America, Africa, and Asia. IFPRI warns that this damage to soil substantially reduces

Dust rises as a farmer plows a field in California. Critics of conventional farming claim that the practice has lead to severe soil degradation.

The Promise of Biotechnology

Agribusiness corporations point to exciting new developments in biotechnology as a way to help to limit the number of pesticides applied to foods and make industrial foods healthier. Monsanto, for example, has genetically engineered crops such as corn and cotton, infusing them with a gene from a soil bacterium, Bacillus thuringiensis, a natural type of insecticide used by organic farmers for insect infestations. The company claims this helps to deter pests without applying large quantities of chemical insecticides. Future developments, supporters say, will produce foods that taste better and are enriched with vitamins to make them healthier. As Monsanto's Web site states,

"The benefits of biotechnology, today and in the future, are nearly limitless." Critics, however, say that scientists do not know the long-term health effects of genetically modified (GM) foods and warn that GM crops can spread throughout the environment, contaminating native plants or organic farms. Critics also say GM foods give corporations global control over world food supplies because they own the patents; Monsanto, for example, has sued organic farmers whose crops were contaminated by GM strains, claiming patent infringement. Despite these concerns, GM foods have now been introduced around the world.

agricultural productivity and yields and may even lead to worldwide food shortages in coming decades.

Chemical pesticide use on farms, meanwhile, is rapidly polluting surrounding lands and water systems. In fact, most chemical pesticides applied to crops are not used by the plants themselves, but instead run off into the soil, evaporate into the air, or seep into the ground water. As Cornell University agriculture and ecology professor David Pimentel explains, "Only 0.1 percent of applied pesticides reach the target pests, leaving the bulk of the pesticides (99.9 percent) to impact the environment."[28] One result, according to a 2000 report the environmental group Worldwatch, is that toxic chemicals now contaminate groundwater in every country, endangering the world's precious supplies of freshwater and contributing to a world-wide water crisis. The Food and Agriculture Organization of the United Nations (FAO) urges the use of organic and similar farming methods in order to reduce soil and water degradation. In some countries such as Germany, governments have even begun paying farmers to adopt organic farming practices as a way to preserve clean water supplies.

THE GIANT PESTICIDE INDUSTRY

"The approximately $35-billion-a-year pesticide business ... is dominated by ten corporate giants based in the United States and Western Europe that control nearly 90 percent of the global pesticide market, and this industry is directly responsible for the release of several billion pounds of pesticides into the environment every year."

—Monica Moore, co-director of Pesticide Action Network (PAN) North America, a public interest organization that works to replace chemical pesticides with ecologically sound alternatives.

Monica Moore, "Hidden Dimensions of Damage," *Fatal Harvest: The Tragedy of Industrial Agriculture*, Andrew Kimbrell, ed., Washington, D.C.: Island Press, 2002, p. 255.

Agricultural Chemicals Damage Plants and Wildlife

The overload of chemical fertilizers and pesticides in the air, soil, and water also affects whole ecosystems, often poisoning natural habitats and harming or killing birds, wild animals, and beneficial insects, and destroying biodiversity. Professor David Pimentel estimates, for example, that pesticides kill approximately 67 million birds each year in the United States alone. In addition, as scientist Jane Goodall explains:

> Agricultural chemicals ... that enter the rivers and oceans weaken the immune system of dolphins, whales, and thousands of other aquatic creatures. They cause birth defects in frogs and other amphibians—such as hind legs that are fused together or extra legs sprouting form their bellies or backs.[29]

A man paddles through thick duckweed in a river. The explosion of duckweed is thought to be the result of fertilizer runoff from farmlands.

Chemical fertilizers, especially nitrogen and phosphorus, may pose an even bigger threat than pesticides to plants and wildlife. Marine life is the most vulnerable, because fertilizers flow into rivers, lakes, estuaries, and coastal waters, where they encourage the growth of algae that can literally suffocate and kill off fish, plants, and other native aquatic species—a process known as eutrophication in freshwaters and algal bloom in oceans. As organic farmer Jason McKenny explains:

> Every summer, rains carry eroded soils and fertilizer run-off out of Midwestern fields draining 1.2 million square miles of watershed into the Mississippi River, down to the Gulf of Mexico.... A huge dead zone, at time encompassing the whole water column, forms off the coast of the delta estuary.... The estuaries of the Chesapeake, Massachusetts, North Carolina, San Francisco Bay, and numerous others all regularly experience the ecological destruction this runoff brings.[30]

A 2003 report from the Pew Oceans Commission confirms this assessment. It found that polluted nutrient runoff from U.S. farms and cities over the past 30 years—primarily nitrogen fertilizers—is severely damaging U.S. coastal waters and making them uninhabitable for fish and native plants. Excess nitrogen also pollutes drinking water and escapes into the atmosphere, where it transforms into nitrous oxides—a greenhouse gas that contributes to ozone depletion and climate change.

The huge tracts of monoculture farmland operated by industrial agriculture corporations, too, have been criticized for destroying natural habitat and dramatically reducing the number of wildlife populations. Thousands of species of wild plants and animals in the U.S. Midwest, including important game species such as prairie chickens, bobwhite quail, cottontail rabbits, and ring-necked pheasants, have been greatly reduced in number or lost completely. As environmental activist Andrew Kimbrell explains, "Planting thousand-acre fields of corn ... leaves virtually no room for the propagation of other species."[31]

FEEDING THE WORLD WITH ORGANIC FOOD

"Organic farming can feed about 3 billion people, not the 6 billion that we now have, or the 9 billion that we will have."
—San Diego Center for Molecular Agriculture, a group of university and biotechnology scientists working in the San Diego, California area.

San Diego Center for Molecular Agriculture, "Foods from Genetically Modified Crops," San Diego, CA, undated. www.sdcma.org/publications2.html.

Many environmentalists believe the overall damage caused by conventional agriculture is a true global catastrophe. As research scientist Catherine Badgley puts it:

For the first time in 65 million years, the world is in the early phases of a mass extinction, this one resulting from human impacts on the biosphere. Agriculture, more than any other human activity, has the greatest collective negative effect on Earth's biodiversity.[32]

However, the environmental costs of industrial farming are not added to the prices paid by consumers for conventional food, nor factored into corporate business or profit calculations.

Amish Farms

Some of the most productive farms in the United States are those owned by the Amish, a Christian religious sect of Swiss and German ancestry living in the northeastern United States and Canada. The Amish are known for their rejection of modern dress and customs, and more traditional Amish groups, called "old order Amish," refuse to use technological conveniences such as electricity and automobiles. For religious reasons, the Amish have clung to their traditional way of life, emphasizing family, community, and a rural, agricultural lifestyle. For more than a hundred years, Amish families have farmed large tracts of land in states like Pennsylvania and Ohio using traditional farming techniques developed long before the advent of industrial agriculture. Many still plow their fields with horse-drawn equipment. Although a few Amish farmers use a limited amount of chemical fertilizers and pesticides, most Amish families have been farming organically—using manure fertilizers, techniques such as crop rotation and cover crops, and pasture-raising their animals—since before the "organic" term was developed. Today, these farms are still highly productive, and many are reaping the rewards of the growing interest in organic food. Amish farmers, once viewed as holdouts of the nineteenth century, are now seen by many as the example to be followed.

Instead, organic advocates say, conventional food prices are kept artificially low, while the environmental costs of conventional farming are passed on to the public in the form of government grants and support for farmers, environmental cleanups, and increased health care costs. Including these environmental costs, a 2004 study by Iowa State University economists found that the true costs of U.S. agriculture to taxpayers are at least $5 to $16 billion each year. As reporter Christy Harrison puts it, "We're paying a lot in taxes in order to pay a pittance at the grocery store."[33]

Environmental Benefits of Organic Farming

Organic advocates say organic farming provides a stark contrast to the destruction caused by industrial farming, because it works in harmony with nature and promotes sustainability and biodiversity. Organic techniques, such as planting many different kinds of crops, retaining landscape diversity, and including patches of natural vegetation alongside farmed fields, help to support native plants and animal species. In addition, many organic farmers avoid excessive tilling of the soil as much as possible.

To organic farmers, the soil is alive, part of Mother Earth, a carefully balanced mix of materials teeming with tiny organisms and nutrients that must be carefully managed to ensure fertility and plant growth. Organic farmers' soil conservation efforts not only help crops to grow, however; they also help the environment by decreasing the need for fertilizers and pesticides. And because synthetic chemicals are not used for fertilizing and controlling pests, organic farming produces less pollution in the soil, water, and air than conventional farming methods. Less pollution, in turn, makes organic farms safer for agricultural and other food workers, and provides non-toxic habitats for birds and other wild creatures.

Studies have also suggested that organic farms use less energy, create less waste, and thus are more efficient than industrial farms. Conventional farms require large amounts of energy, including the energy required to make chemical fertilizers and pesticides and also to power large tractors and other farm machinery. In contrast, Professor David Pimentel found that U.S. organic farms use just 63 percent of the energy required by conventional farming systems. A 2003 study by the Rodale Institute reached similar results, finding that organic farming uses 50 percent less energy than conventional agriculture. And almost everything on an organic farm is recycled back into the soil, preventing waste.

In addition, organic agriculture techniques such as mulching, composting, and crop diversity help organic soils to contain more humus and retain more water—a characteristic that makes organic farms more resilient during periods of high temperatures and reduced rainfall or drought. Organic soils, too, absorb water faster during periods of intense rain, helping to

A worker plants seeds on Honey Brook Organic Farm in New Jersey. Organic farms are thought to be more energy efficient than conventional farms.

avoid flooding. Experts say these advantages should mean that organic agriculture will more easily cope with future global warming changes. According to Louise Luttikholt, a manager at the International Federation of Organic Agriculture Movements (IFOAM) in Germany, for example, a village in northern Ethiopia that converted to organic agriculture continued to harvest crops even during a severe drought, while neighboring villages using industrial farming methods lost their crops. As Luttikholt explains, "Organic agriculture is about optimising yields under all conditions."[34]

Organic farming, according to supporters, can even help reduce greenhouse gas emissions that cause global warming. A 15-year "Farming Systems Trial" conducted by the Rodale Institute monitored carbon and nitrogen levels in soils of organic and conventional farms and found that carbon increased in the organic systems by 15 to 28 percent while there was little change in non-organic systems. The study, published in 2003, concluded that organic agriculture reduces greenhouse gas emissions by capturing carbon in the soil, where it stimulates plant growth. The study showed that if just 10,000 medium-sized farms in the U.S. converted to organic production, they would reduce carbon levels about as much as taking 1,174,400 cars off the road. Anthony Rodale, chairman of the Rodale Institute, argues, "Organic farming is a powerful new tool in the global warming arsenal.... It puts agriculture into a lead role in regenerating the environment."[35]

Indeed, supporters of organic agriculture believe organic methods must be adopted in place of conventional farming techniques in order to save the planet from environmental destruction. Many environmental experts agree with this conclusion. A 2002 report by the Food and Agriculture Organization of the United Nations (FAO), for example, found that organic agriculture is good for the world environment on all levels. The report concluded, "Organic agriculture counteracts resource depletion (soil, water, energy, nutrients), contributes positively to the problems associated with climate change ... and can help to maintain and enhance biodiversity at a global scale."[36] The FAO urged that organic practices be adopted by small farmers around the world, both to conserve natural resources and to ensure regional food security.

Environmental Costs of Organic Farming

On the other hand, critics charge that organic food may be no better for the environment than conventional agriculture. Although organic farmers do not use synthetic pesticides, they do employ many organic pesticides—that is, pesticides derived from natural products that are permitted under government regulations. In fact, some reports claim that these natural pesticides make up more than 25 percent of the total pesticide use in the United States. As Alex Avery of the non-profit Center For Global Food Issues contends, "Organic pesticides are the most heavily used agricultural pesticides in the U.S."[37]

According to critics, some of these organic pesticides can be more environmentally toxic than synthetic pesticides. As Tech News staff writer Alex Knapp explains:

> Two of the most common organic pesticides, copper and sulfur, are used as fungicides by organic growers. Because they are not as effective as their synthetic counterparts, they are applied at significantly higher rates. This is disturbing because both sulfur and copper have greater environmental toxicity than their synthetic counterparts.[38]

Similarly, chemist Nancy McGuire argues, "Many of these [natural pesticide] compounds are toxic to fish, and they persist in the soil longer than currently used synthetic pesticides."[39] Also, Knapp explains, "One ...pesticide [derived from plants], pyrethrum, has a demand satisfied by the hand harvest of about 600 million flowers per year. This accounts for a significant amount of green space that could otherwise be used as wildlife preserve or to grow food."[40] Moreover, biological pesticides—that is, using insects, fungi, or bacteria to attack pests—can introduce non-native organisms into local ecosystems, sometimes with devastating results.

Organics Require More Land and More Energy

In addition, critics say many organic products require far more land or take longer to grow than the same conventional products, so they actually use more energy, create higher carbon emissions, and contribute more significantly to global warming than the same conventional products. A 2007 report issued by Britain's Department for Environment, Food and Rural Affairs bolstered this view. The report confirmed that many organic products produced less environmental damage than conventionally grown products, but it found that these positive environmental effects were offset by other organic foods that cause more pollution than their conventional counterparts. Researchers in the British study found, for example, that:

British researchers found that although the production of organic milk requires less energy, it requires more land than conventional production.

organic milk production appears to require less energy input but much more land than conventional production. While eliminating pesticide use, it also gives rise to higher emissions of greenhouse gases and eutrophying substances [that produce damaging algae growth in water systems].[41]

Results were similar for other organic foods. Organic chickens, for instance, were found to take longer to grow and therefore to use more energy and cause more pollution. And organic tomatoes were found to require almost ten times the amount of land and double the amount of energy as conventional tomatoes.

Moreover, organic foods, like conventionally grown foods, are increasingly shipped around the globe, and those transportation activities—often referred to as "food miles"—add to carbon emissions that cause global warming and environmental ills. As environmental management professor Ken Green, who co-wrote the British report, explained:

> You cannot say that all organic food is better for the environment than all food grown conventionally. If you look carefully at the amount of energy required to produce these foods you get a complicated picture. In some cases, the carbon footprint for organics is larger.[42]

Other organic critics focus on the environmental impact of the large amounts of land necessary for organic production. Dennis T. Avery, for example, argues:

> The Green Revolution allowed the world to save at least 15 million square miles of wildlands from being plowed for low-yield food production. Think of it in these terms: high-yield farming has saved wildlands equal to the total land area of the United States, Europe, and South America combined.[43]

Converting to organic production, Avery says, would mean that "the world would immediately have to clear at least 10 million square miles of wildlands for green manure crops like clover and rye."[44] Nor is organic farming socially beneficial for many people employed in the industry. Critics point out that although farm owners may be reaping profits from the growth of the organic markets, the farm workers who harvest organic produce do back-breaking work, such as hand-weeding to avoid using pesticides, in jobs that are very low paying and offer few, if any, benefits.

Feeding a Hungry World

Organic critics also say organic farming will not produce enough food at low enough prices to feed the starving world, especially not a world population that is expected to grow from today's 6.5 billion to 9 billion by 2050. First, as critics point out, organic food is much more expensive than conventionally grown foods, largely because organic farmers rely on labor-intensive farming methods, such as hand-picking, rather than highly mechanized methods used by large industrial farms. As the organic market grows, many experts expect organic prices to decrease. Thomas Dobbs, a sustainable-agriculture economist at South Dakota State University, for example, predicts that if just one-third of American shoppers bought organic foods on a regular basis, most organic prices would come down 10 to 30 percent,

Critics of organic farming point out that organic food is more expensive than conventionally grown food because of the labor-intensive methods that organic farmers. use.

putting them at about at same price levels as conventional foods. Nobody knows when that price decline will occur, however, and in the meantime, many people are unable to pay the higher prices for organically grown foods. Critics of the organic approach say, therefore, that organic food is affordable only for the wealthy and not a viable option for most consumers, especially the very poor.

In addition, critics say organic farmers cannot produce the same amounts of food as conventional farms that use chemicals and intensive farming methods. By any measure, agricultural yields have increased dramatically in the last several decades, and as Dennis T. Avery notes, "Plant breeding, chemical nitrogen fertilizer, irrigation, and pesticides have been critical to this massive high-yield ... triumph."[45] Experts say farm output will have to increase significantly by the year 2050 in order to feed the world's growing population, and critics contend organic farms simply cannot match the efficiency already shown by industrial farming. Some critics say that, at best, organic agriculture is capable of producing only about 50 percent of the yield of conventional agriculture.

The reason for lower yields in organic food production, critics say, is that organic farmers face certain practical limitations. British plant biologist Anthony Trewavas, for example, argues that it would be impossible to produce enough animal manure to fertilize crops to feed the world, and replacing soil nutrients with other natural fertilizers or through cover crops alone would not work. Also, biological control of insects and diseases is not as efficient as chemical pesticides. Other inefficiencies of organic food production include its dependence on manual labor and the amount of land needed for organic production.

Researchers Disagree About Organic Yields

Some research supports the claim of lower organic yields. A Swiss study, reported in 2002, for example, found that organic farming produced about 20 percent less than conventional farms. Although organic plots produced healthier soils and used less energy, the organic wheat yields in the Swiss tests averaged only 4 tons per hectare, compared to the national wheat average

Researchers have found that corn is just one of four major organic crops that meets or exceeds conventional farm yields for those same crops.

of 6 to 7 tons per hectare. Similarly, the organic potatoes yielded only about 3 tons per hectare, compared to a national average of more than 4 tons per hectare. Trevawas said of the study, "The poor yields achieved by the Swiss organic plots mean that organic farming in the real world could not feed our expected peak population without plowing down huge tracts of wildlife habitat."[46]

Organic supporters, however, reject these arguments and claim that organic farming actually produces equivalent or bigger yields than conventional agriculture. Organic agriculture, they point out, produces more fertile soils so yields are usually good and food quality is high. Some studies support this argument as well. A study of apple farming by researchers at Washington State University, published in 2001, for example, found that organic orchards can be more profitable and produce tastier fruit while producing yields similar to those at conventional apple farms. Another study, publicized in 2003 by scientists from the University of Minnesota, found that yields of organic corn and soybeans were only slightly below production levels for conventional produce. In the study, conducted between 1993 and 1999, organically grown corn yields averaged between 9 and 7 percent less than conventional corn, while organic soybeans averaged between 19 and 16 percent less than conventional soybean crops. The Organic Consumers Association says this study shows that "organic production practices ... offer an alternative to conventional [farming] practices."[47]

Bill Liebhardt, a sustainable agriculture specialist at the University of California at Davis, surveyed both academic research and the experience of individual organic farmers over the past ten years, and found that organic agriculture matches the yields of conventional farms for all types of crops. Liebhardt found that academic field studies of four major crops—corn, soybeans, wheat, and tomatoes—showed that organic yields fell between 94 and 100 percent of conventional yields, and yields realized by real-world organic farms met or exceeded conventional farm yields for those same crops. In addition, Liebhardt argues:

> What these yield figures do not reflect are the other benefits derived by organic producers and the land: increased profit per acre and improved soil quality as measured by soil structure, organic matter, biological activity, water infiltration, and water-holding capacity. This translates to higher yields during drought under organic systems, leading to production stability year after year. Nitrogen leaching is reduced considerably under organic agriculture, leading to less water pollution—a major ecological issue all over the world.[48]

As the competing claims about agricultural yields show, although many experts see a clear connection between organic agriculture and a cleaner environment, there still is great controversy about whether the world can or should abandon industrial agriculture and adopt organic or more natural farming methods.

THE FUTURE OF ORGANIC FOOD PRODUCTION

The organic food industry is expected to continue to grow in the future, and this prospect generates both hopes and fears about how it will evolve. Many organic advocates hope that organic growth will ultimately replace today's conventional agricultural system with one that will not only improve current organic values but also embrace broader environmental and social goals. Organic supporters, however, worry that the entry of large, multinational corporations into the organic market may ultimately change organic food production in ways that will dilute national standards, eliminate small-scale organic farmers, and destroy the industry's commitment to food safety and the environment. Whatever the outcome, most experts agree that some form of organic food will likely be part of the future.

Predictions of a Growth Industry

Virtually all projections suggest that the organic food industry will continue to grow in future years, in the United States as well as the rest of the world. Currently, there is more demand than supply in some places. According to the Organic Trade Association (OTA), however, the future industry growth rate may slow to something less than the current 15 to 20 percent average annual growth rate in sales, perhaps somewhere nearer 5 to 10 percent per year. Even at this rate, however, organic sales could easily reach $50 billion per year by 2025, a figure that would represent nearly 6 percent of all U.S. food sales.

OTA says that in the future, the average consumer will buy all kinds of organic products on a regular basis, and these will include not only food, but also clothing, household cleaning products, and personal care items. The OTA also expects U.S.

Cuba's Organic Food System

Today, organic food is grown throughout the world. One country—the socialist island nation Cuba that lies just to the south of the United States—adopted organic agriculture by necessity after its close ally and supporter, the Soviet Union, began to collapse economically and politically in 1989. The Soviet disintegration ended critical food support to Cuba, including heavily subsidized fertilizers and pesticides on which its agriculture system was long dependent. Cuba could not import these items from the United States because of a U.S. trade embargo that prohibits any exchange of goods between the countries. Facing food shortages, Cuba abandoned its intensive industrial agriculture model and embraced small-scale organic and similar types of farming. This new system includes small urban gardens grown by residents of Cuba's capital city of Havana, called "Huertos Populares" (popular gardens), as well as larger farms run by small farmers or the government. According to experts who have studied Cuba's agriculture, this new farming system helped the country to overcome its food shortages by mid-1995, and many of the small farms have even experienced increased yields with organic methods. Today, these gardens and farms are thriving and serve as a model for other developing countries.

and world organic farmland to increase significantly, from the current 1 percent to somewhere around 8 to 15 percent, as more and more farmers switch to organic methods. All this growth in the organic industry, OTA says, will require increased government support, both enforcement of organic standards and assistance to help farmers make the transition from conventional farming to organic methods.

Beyond Organic

Many organic advocates predict that the interest in organically grown food will bring with it a change in people's values. As environmentalist and sustainable farming advocate Jim Slama explains:

For many farmers and consumers, organic represents the values that are most important to them. It is food with a mission—representing care for the earth, compassion for animals, commitment to social justice, and support for local farms and communities. In coming years, organic agriculture will embrace these values in a more defined way.[49]

Slama and others hope that these changing values will one day lead to a truly sustainable world food system that will produce safe and healthy food, protect the environment, minimize food miles, treat animals humanely, provide jobs to support local economies, and reinvigorate family farms.

WANING ORGANIC STANDARDS

"As the organic food industry has matured, USDA standards have waned. Consumers can no longer be confidant that their foods meet organic standards, even if USDA gives its green mark of approval."

—Joshua Frank, author and organic advocate.

Joshua Frank, "Federal Food Policy: Organic Inconsistencies," *Jackson Progressive*, December, 2005. www.jacksonprogressive.com/issues/foodtech/organicinconsistencies121805.html.

As a first step, organic supporters would like to see U.S. organic standards expanded to include some of these environmental, moral, and social values. The U.S. government's current standards for organic foods, many people argue, are primarily concerned with prohibiting synthetic chemical inputs into organic products, and do not adequately protect the environment, workers, or animals. Already, a number of companies are adding additional information to their "USDA Organic" in order to attract interest from consumers. As Sarah Miles, marketing director at New Leaf Community Markets in Santa Cruz, California, explains:

As the organic industry changes, people are beginning to realize there are different values served by different

A shirt made with organic fibers. Organic advocates predict that the interest in organic food will not only change the way people eat, but also change people's values.

choices.... Consumers and retailers who want products with ecologically friendly attributes like locally grown, fairly traded or humanely or sustainably produced are spawning a new movement that has been dubbed 'beyond organic.[50]

The two most popular labels that go beyond the current USDA organic standards are "locally grown" and "fair trade." Locally grown refers to products grown close to their final market destination—a practice that supporters say ensures food freshness and avoids shipping products long distances, thereby using less fossil fuels that cause damage to the environment. Fair trade is a designation designed to assure consumers that farmers who produce the food product have been fairly compensated for their labor. "Fair Trade Certified," for example, means that the certifying organization, Trans Fair USA, has verified that the product has been grown by small farmers who received a fair minimum price for their crops and that the buyer has paid 60 percent of this price in advance. Consumer interest in these new labels is exploding. As Ronnie Cummins, founder of the Organic Consumers Association, explains:

> Fair-trade products are growing even faster than organic in Western nations.... And another trend that is very big now is to buy local. There's real synergy now with these ideas and the organic movement. We have a perfect storm of massive marketplace interest in new ideas.[51]

Other labels that may gain ground in the future are those that promise a company's commitment to ideals such as environmentally sound and sustainable agriculture, small-scale farming, biological diversity, and raising livestock humanely.

Some organic leaders believe these "beyond organic" concepts may eventually be incorporated into mandatory organic standards. As consumers become more and more concerned

Criticism of "Fair Trade" Labeling

The idea of "Fair Trade" labeling—to provide a living wage to farmers—sounds like an idea no one could disagree with, but some economists argue it has many drawbacks. The main argument against fair trade is that it encourages higher prices than what the market would otherwise produce. Critics say when items such as coffee are overproduced, prices naturally should drop, and that in turn should encourage producers to switch to growing other products. Instead, fair trade labeling acts as a subsidy that raises the price for coffee, encouraging more producers to enter the market. In addition, critics argue that guaranteeing premium prices removes the incentive for farmers to improve quality or learn how to compete in the global market. Yet another criticism of fair trade products is that they do not provide farmers a very big share of the price mark-up, and that most of the premium charged goes to retailers who sell the product. Also, the 2005 entry of the giant food corporation, Nestle, into the fair trade coffee market, many say, is proof that the fair trade market will soon be just another marketing strategy for big business.

In 2003, Back to Nature was purchased by Kraft. This is just one in a long list of examples of small organic companies being purchased by large corporations.

about the environment and the related social and moral issues of food production, corporations may realize that they must become more environmentally and socially responsible, if only to improve sales and stay in business. Other commentators think these new labels will likely remain voluntary, and be used mostly by smaller organic farmers as a way to market their goods, leaving the larger, more industrial organic companies to focus on foods that meet only minimum organic standards. As environmental author Michael Pollan explains,

> I see that industrial organics will only get bigger.... The farmers who realize they can no longer compete in that environment realize that they can grow food better for new channels of distribution. There is room for both. Some will be selling better social values, some more humane treatment of animals. There are all kinds of ways to align the market with nature, and that's especially true with food.[52]

Corporate Takeover of the Organic Industry

Still other organic supporters increasingly fear that the whole organic movement may be co-opted by companies concerned mainly about profits. Today, for example, the biggest concern about the organic market's future involves the effect of giant corporations buying up organic food labels, taking power away from dedicated and idealistic consumers and the small organic farmers who nurtured and established the industry. The list of small organic companies that have been purchased by big corporate interests is now quite long, with no end in sight. For example: General Mills now owns the organic companies Cascadian Farm and Muir Glen; Kellogg owns Kashi, Morningstar Farms, and Sunrise Organic; Coca-Cola owns Odwalla; Kraft owns Boca Burgers and Back to Nature; Unilever owns Ben & Jerry's; and Heinz owns Hain, Breadshop, Arrowhead Mills, Celestial Seasonings, and numerous other popular organic brands. These big corporate interests see the rapidly growing consumer organic market and the higher price points of organic products and want to share those profits. Already, big business controls a significant portion of the organic industry. In California, for example, about 27 large organic companies representing only 2 percent of all the state's organic farms reportedly are responsible for over half of the state's organic sales.

Some experts applaud this corporate interest in the organic market, because they see it as a sign that organic foods will become mainstream and eventually lead to a cleaner environment. As organic expert Michael Sligh puts it, "Every acre that is legitimately converted to organic is an acre where you're not polluting the soil or contaminating the groundwater or spraying toxic pesticides on workers."[53] Many of these big corporations, however, are closely connected with industrial agriculture and even with the companies that produce most of the chemical fertilizers and pesticides used around the world—interests that have always been hostile to organic farming ideals. Some of the biggest stockholders of General Mills, for example, include Monsanto, DuPont, and Dow Chemical—all powerful manufacturers of chemical agricultural products.

Critics say it is no surprise, therefore, that many of the multinational companies taking over organic farmland are rejecting tenets long held by smaller organic farmers, most notably their commitment to sustainable soils, biodiversity, and the environment. These big organic farms may not use chemical pesticides or genetically modified seeds, but many of them still rely on industrial agriculture methods that do not seek harmony with nature or protect the environment. Instead of using manure and compost techniques to build up soil fertility, for example, many large farm operators apply pre-packaged organic fertilizers to give it a temporary jolt. Instead of growing a variety of crops and rotating them to conserve the soil, they are mass-producing monoculture crops just as in conventional agriculture. They also are using large amounts of water and energy, choosing excessive packaging, and shipping products for long distances. As organic supporter Jane Goodall explains, "In California, where growing conditions are ideal almost all year-round, there are huge organic farms producing just one variety of carrot or vast fields

Organic supporter Jane Goodall explains that the new corporate approach to organic is often called "shallow organic" because the process the corporations use does not adhere to the core values of the organic movement.

of romaine lettuce that are eventually shipped cross-country in sealed plastic bags."[54]

Indeed, the organic industry is quickly being globalized by multinational corporate owners: increasingly, organic foods found in U.S. supermarkets and organic food stores comes from huge organic farms in distant places such as Mexico, Central and South America, and even China. Current organic standards do not prevent this, but many organic supporters see it as a violation of basic organic values. As Mark Kastel, head of the Cornucopia Institute, explains, "Shipping our food around the world and burning fossil fuels, that's not organic.... That might be technically organic, but it's not what people think they're paying for."[55] Goodall explains that this new corporate approach to organic production is often called "shallow organic:" The end products may technically win an organic label, but they are destructive to many of the core values of the early organic movement.

The Threat to Organic Standards

Critics say the corporate takeover of organic production is slowly eroding the grass-roots network of small organic producers in the United States who were committed to maintaining high standards for consumers. And many of the new corporate owners of organic brands have strong influence over policymakers such as the president, Congress, and the regulatory agencies that monitor organic agriculture. Organic advocates fear that these corporations will use their influence to dilute and weaken the federal definition of organic and the current organic regulations to make organic production similar to industrial farming.

In fact, critics say President George W. Bush and his appointees at the USDA—all closely connected to powerful agribusiness interests—have already sought to undermine U.S. organic standards in a variety of ways. According to the environmental advocacy group Center for Food Safety (CFS), the Bush administration sought to change organic standards in the first year after organic standards were adopted. The attempted changes included placing new chemicals on the list of substances approved for organic use, allowing unapproved additives to be used in processing organic foods, and eliminating outdoor access requirements for poultry. In addition, CFS claims Bush appointees sought to eliminate the requirement that livestock feed be 100 percent organic, and tried to force small-scale, farmer-based organic certifiers out of the organic program. Later, in 2004, the USDA considered relaxing organic certification standards to allow the use of sewage sludge fertilizers, GMOs, and irradiated processing methods. The USDA also wanted to allow organic animal producers to retain their organic certification even if they used animal growth hormones and said seafood, pet food, and body care products could use "organic" on their labels without meeting any standards at all. Only an avalanche of letters from angry consumers and organic farmers prevented these changes. CFS warned at that time, "If the Bush administration's current policies are continued, the integrity of all organic food could be fatally compromised, and this crucial alternative to industrial agriculture would be lost."[56]

In 2005, some of the worst fears of organic supporters were realized when, despite receiving more than 350,000 letters from the organic community, Republican leaders in Congress successfully attached an amendment to the 2006 Agricultural Appropriations that weakened national organic standards. According to the Organic Consumers Association (OCA), the amendment allows: Numerous new synthetic food additives and processing aids to be used in organic foods without public review; young dairy cows to be treated with antibiotics and fed genetically engineered feed prior to being converted to organic production; and the substitution of non-organic ingredients for organic ingredients without any notification of the public based on "emergency decrees." These changes were the result of pressure from big industrial agriculture interests. As the OCA explains:

> Agribusiness front groups, such as the Farm Bureau, big food corporations like Kraft, biotech companies such as Monsanto, right-wing think tanks, such as the Hudson Institute, and industry-friendly government agencies have consistently tried to undermine organic standards

and get the USDA to allow conventional chemical-intensive and factory farm practices on organic farms. Unless strict organic standards are maintained, consumers will lose faith in the organic label.[57]

Other problems have been documented with the lack of government enforcement of organic standards. An investigation by the *Dallas Morning News* in 2006, for example, found that hundreds of complaints have been filed with the USDA and audits of organic certifiers show many violations, but the government has never suspended a certifier's accreditation. As Jim Riddle, former chairman of NOSB and advisor to USDA, reported to the newspaper, "The USDA has failed to enforce the regulations....

In order for a dairy farm to be considered organic, the cows must be allowed to have access to a pasture like the one picured here at the Alisa Farm in Wisconsin.

There have been no prosecutions [for] violations [of] the organic law yet."[58] Instead, watchdog groups are leading the fight against organic violations. The Organic Consumers Association, for example, is encouraging consumers to boycott Horizon and Aurora dairy products as well as two leading organic soy products, Silk and White Wave, charging that these companies are:

> continuing to sell milk and dairy products labeled as 'USDA Organic,' even though most or all of their milk is coming from factory farm feedlots where the animals have been brought in from conventional farms and are kept in intensive confinement, with little or no access to pasture.[59]

Horizon and Aurora defended their farming practices, claiming their cows spend several months per year in an outside pasture.

Future Changes to Organic Standards

The USDA is also studying several other possible changes to the U.S. organic rules that concern organic supporters. One issue is whether and how to certify fish products as organic. Currently, there is no official U.S. organic label for seafood, and the USDA is investigating how to ensure that fish get an organic diet. Farmed fish—that is, fish and seafood grown in open-water net pens, natural ponds, or fully enclosed land-based water systems and fed processed fish food—can be fairly easily be limited to an organic diet. The diet of wild fish, however, cannot be controlled, and many wild fish are contaminated with dangerous pollutants such as Polychlorinated biphenyls (PCBs), which can build up in the human body and cause serious reproductive and other health effects. In addition, even if farmed fish are fed organic food, and not treated with antibiotics or other non-organic substances, critics say fish farming is destructive to the environment. The unnatural grouping of large number of fish, for example, produce fish diseases and concentrations of wastes that can pollute or destroy local marine habitats. Some of these farmed fish have also escaped from their pens, and have preyed on and destroyed or diminished native fish populations.

Organic and environmental advocates are concerned about how this issue will be decided by the USDA.

Another brewing controversy has to do with whether cloned animals or their offspring could be considered organic under federal standards. The FDA announced in December 2006 that it plans to approve food from cloned animals. The current U.S. organic standards, however, do not mention cloning, although they exclude genetically engineered items from being considered organic. The USDA so far has taken the position that cloned animals cannot be sold as organic, but biotechnology company have indicated that they want the government to allow the progeny of cloned animals to be permitted in organic products. They point out that the FDA has already determined that cloning is not genetic engineering, since cloning leaves the gene sequence intact and merely duplicates it, and they argue that cloning is simply a way to help animals reproduce, similar to artificial insemination or other technologies already used by animal producers. Organic supporters worry that the USDA may eventually be pressured to accept this pro-cloning point of view.

Organic Farming Around the World

Whatever the future of organic farming in the United States, organic and other forms of more sustainable agriculture are increasingly being adopted around the world. Westernized countries such as Germany, Britain, and Australia have vigorous organic industries similar to the U.S. organic market. In addition, many poorer, developing countries are rejecting industrial farming methods and beginning to see organic farming as a solution to their problems of poverty and hunger. After decades of industrial agriculture that promised to feed the world, world hunger is still on the increase, prompting leaders of some of the poorest countries to search for alternatives.

Indeed, supporters say organic methods seem particularly well-suited to poorer, less-developed countries. Because it is so labor intensive, for example, organic agriculture can provide jobs that do not require much education and make use of local people's traditional farming knowledge to help to lift people out of poverty. Organic methods also free developing governments from dependence on chemicals, hybrid seeds, and technical advice from Western corporations—a dependence created by industrial agriculture systems. And organic farming provides a way to produce healthy food locally and feed the hungry without destroying valuable soil and water supplies or causing other environmental harm.

In India, for example, organic farming is experiencing what Volkert Engelsman, the CEO of a European organic distribution company, calls "explosive growth."[60] Like many other developing nations, India was faced with a rising population, rapidly depleting soils, water shortages, and high costs for the chemicals and other inputs necessary to maintain its industrial agriculture system. These problems caused the country to rethink its agriculture policy and move towards more environmentally-

Many third-world countries are adopting the practices of organic farming, like raising free-range chickens, as a solution to their problems of poverty and hunger.

friendly, less costly, and locally-based farming methods. As Engelsman argues, "It is more economically sustainable to invest in the soils of your land than to make the chemical companies richer."[61] Well-known Indian scientist and environmentalist Vandana Shiva also favors organic agriculture, because she believes its high yields will help India to develop a more secure and sustainable food supply than industrial methods. The idea that organic agriculture is better for developing countries also is gaining acceptance in other parts of the globe, from Brazil to the Philippines. As Engelsman puts it, "Everyone is embracing organic agriculture now."[62]

Organic agriculture and other forms of non-chemical farming thus appear to have a bright future, both in Westernized countries such as the United States as well as in less developed parts of the world. This expansion of organic agriculture will directly challenge the system of industrial agriculture that has dominated American and world agriculture for many decades. However, few experts predict that organic farming will completely replace conventional, chemical-based farming, if only because the rapidly rising world population may eclipse the ability of organic farms to acquire enough fertile land to produce adequate amounts of food to meet demand. Some commentators, therefore, think that it is more likely for organic and conventional farming to merge into a variety of farming systems—some completely organic, others a mixture of organic methods and minimal chemical use, and still others continuing to resemble today's conventional farms. Farmers may simply choose the best methods to fit their needs and produce enough food for their region, perhaps with an increased emphasis on protecting the natural environment

At the moment, the organic industry is still in its infancy, its very definition and standards subject to the outcome of the struggle between commercial interests and consumers' values. As this struggle is resolved, organic foods and similar products may increasingly be available to anyone who wants them, whether for health, social, cost, moral, or environmental reasons.

Introduction: Organic Goes Mainstream

1. Laurie Demeritt, "Consumers Drive Organic Mainstream," *Organic Processing,* April-June 2006. www.organicprocessing.com/opaprjune06/opaj06market.htm.

2. *Natural Life,* "Wal-Mart Style Organics," January-February 2007, p. 34.

3. Amanda Paulson, "As 'Organic' Goes Mainstream, Will Standards Suffer?," *Christian Science Monitor*, May 17, 2006. www.csmonitor.com/2006/0517/p13s01-lifo.html.

4. Diane Brady, "The Organic Myth; Pastoral Ideals Are Getting Trampled as Organic Food Goes Mass Market," *Business Week,* October 16, 2006, Iss. 4005, p. 50.

Chapter 1: The Meaning of "Organic"

5. David Joachim and Rochelle Davis, *Fresh Choices*, New York; Rodale, 2004, p. 127.

6. National Center for Appropriate Technology, "CAFOs and AFOs: Definitions and Issues," undated. www.ncat.org/nutrients/hypoxia/cafosdef.htm.

7. Marsha Mason, "Sustainable Agriculture: The Consciousness of Farming," *Green Money Journal,* Spring 2007, Vol. XV, Iss. 3, no. 63. www.greenmoneyjournal.com/article.mpl?newsletterid=39&articleid=508.

8. Steve Diver, "Biodynamic Farming & Compost Preparation," National Sustainable Agriculture Information Service (ATTRA) Publication #IP137, 1999. www.attra.org/attra-pub/biodynamic.html.

9. Quoted in Lawrence Haftl, "Introduction to Masanobu Fukuoka," The Fukuoka Farming Website, November 6, 2005. www.fukuokafarmingol.info/fintro.html.

10. National Organic Board, April 1995, www.ota.com/definition/nosb.html.

11. Joachim and Davis, *Fresh Choices*, New York: Rodale, 2004, p. 126.

Chapter 2: The Rise of the Organic Food Market

12. Illinois State Museum, "The Sadorus Farm," 2006. www.museum. state.il.us/ismdepts/art/sadorus/Sadorus_Farm.html.

13. Deirdre Birmingham, "How Organic is Organic? What the New Federal Regulations Mean for Consumers," *New Life Journal*, June/July 2002. www.newlifejournal.com/junjul02/birmingham. shtml.

14. Natural Resources Defense Council, "The Story of Silent Spring," April 16, 1997. www.nrdc.org/health/pesticides/hcarson.asp.

15. Quoted in Ronald Bailey, "Silent Spring at 40: Rachel Carson's classic Is Not Aging Well," Reason Online, June 12, 2002. www. reason.com/news/show/34823.html.

16. Brian Baker, "Brief History of Organic Farming and the National Organic Program," Organic Farming Compliance Handbook: A Resource Guide for Western Region Agricultural Professionals, University of California Sustainable Agriculture Research and Education Program (SAREP), 2005. www.sarep.ucdavis.edu/organic/complianceguide/.

17. David K. Bowles, "The National Organic Program: Cleaned Up and Ready to Grow," *Agricultural Management Committee Newsletter*, American Bar Association, March 2001, Vol. 5, No. 2.

Chapter 3: Are There Health Benefits to Eating Organic Food?

18. Monsanto, "Who We Are: A Commitment to Agriculture," 2004-2007. www.monsanto.com/monsanto/layout/about_us/default. asp.

19. Environmental Working Group, "Forbidden Fruit: Illegal Pesticides in the U.S. Food Supply," February 1995. www.ewg.org/reports/fruit/chapter2.html.

20. Jane Goodall, *Harvest for Hope: A Guide to Mindful Eating*, New York: Warner Books, 2005, p. 42.

21. Goodall, *Harvest for Hope: A Guide to Mindful Eating*, p. 41.

22. Quoted in FoodNavigator.com, "Organic Foods Have Significantly Fewer Pesticides," August 5, 2002. www.foodnavigator.

com/news/ng.asp?id=43973-organic-foods-have.

23. Mayo Clinic, "Organic Foods: Are They Safer? More Nutritious?," December 20, 2006. www.mayoclinic.com/health/organic-food/NU00255.

24. Quoted in Alex Knapp, "Fallacies and Misconceptions of Organic Foods," Tech News, April 3, 2001.

25. Rob Lyons, "The Truth About Organic Food," Spiked, January 9, 2007. www.spiked-online.com/index.php?/site/article/2691/.

26. Quoted in Farmers Guardian, "Miliband Plays Down the Importance of Organic Food," January 12, 2007.

27. Dennis T. Avery, "The Hidden Dangers in Organic Food," American Outlook, Fall 1998. www.cgfi.org/materials/articles/2002/jun_25_02.htm.

Chapter 4: Organic Farming, The Environment, and Society

28. David Pimentel, "Environmental and Socio-Economic Costs of Pesticide Use," *Techniques for Reducing Pesticide Use*, David Pimentel, ed., New York: John Wiley & Sons, 1997, p. 71.

29. Goodall, *Harvest for Hope: A Guide to Mindful Eating*, p. 41-42.

30. Jason McKenny, "Artificial Fertility," *Fatal Harvest: The Tragedy of Industrial Agriculture*, Andrew Kimbrell, ed., Washington, D.C.: Island Press, 2002, p. 61.

31. Andrew Kimbrell, "Seven Deadly Myths of Industrial Agriculture," *Fatal Harvest: The Tragedy of Industrial Agriculture*, p. 61.

32. Andrew Kimbrell, "Seven Deadly Myths of Industrial Agriculture," *Fatal Harvest: The Tragedy of Industrial Agriculture*, p. 61.

33. Christy Harrison, "The (Still) High Cost of Organic Food," *Grist Magazine*, August 31, 2005. www.alternet.org/envirohealth/24821/.

34. Quoted in Stephen Leahy, "Environment: An Organic Recipe for Development," *Inter Press Service News Agency*, December 18, 2006. http://ipsnews.net/news.asp?idnews=35883.

35. Quoted in AScribe Newswire, "Organic Farming Can Help Reverse Global Warming," October 10, 2003. www.organicconsumers.org/organic/globalwarming101003.cfm.

36. Food and Agriculture Organization of the United Nations, "Or-

ganic Agriculture, Environment and Food Security," Nadia El-Hage Scialabba and Caroline Hattam, eds., 2002. www.fao.org/DOCREP/005/Y4137E/Y4137E00.HTM.

37. Quoted in Knapp, "Fallacies and Misconceptions of Organic Foods," *Tech News*, April 3, 2001.

38. Knapp, "Fallacies and Misconceptions of Organic Foods," *Tech News*, April 3, 2001.

39. Nancy McGuire, "Assessing Organic Food," August 30, 2004. www.chemistry.org/portal/a/c/s/1/feature_pro.html?id=c373e9fe 9f15cae18f6a17245d830100.

40. Knapp, "Fallacies and Misconceptions of Organic Foods," *Tech News,* April 3, 2001.

41. Quoted in Cahal Milmo, "Organic Farming No Better for the Environment," *The Independent*, February 19, 2007. www.thetruthaboutorganicfoods.org/2007/02/20/organic-farming-no-better-for-the-environment/.

42. Quoted in Milmo, "Organic Farming No Better for the Environment."

43. Dennis T. Avery, Commencement Address, University of California, Berkeley, College of Natural Resources, May 21, 2000.

44. Avery, Commencement Address.

45. Dennis T. Avery, Commencement Address.

46. Quoted in Dennis T. Avery, "New Swiss Study Confirms Sharply Lower Yields From Organic Crops," *Center for Global Food Issues*, June 14, 2002. www.cgfi.org/materials/articles/2002/jun_14_ 02.htm.

47. Organic Consumers Association, "Organic Soy and Corn Yields Comparable to Conventional," 2003. www.organicconsumers.org/organic/041903_organic.cfm.

48. Quoted in Elizabeth Ferry, "From the Ground Up: Organic Agriculture Has High Yields and Benefits the Environment," *Co-op Food Stores*, http://www.coopfoodstore.com/news/Archives/arch_ 3-02/ground_up.html.

Chapter 5: The Future of Organic Food Production

49. Jim Slama, "Real Organic--The Food of the Future," Alternet.org, March 28, 2002. www.alternet.org/story.html?StoryID=12732.

50. Quoted in Vicky Uhland, "Retailers Create Value Beyond Organic:

Stores Focusing on Local and Fair Trade Products Find Success," *The Natural Foods Merchandiser*, July 1, 2006. www.transfairusa. org/content/about/n_060701.php.

51. Quoted in Jay Walljasper, "Organic & Beyond: Can Ecology and Commerce Co-exist?," *Ode Magazine*, March 8, 2007. www.organicconsumers.org/articles/article_4457.cfm.

52. Quoted in Jay Walljasper, "Organic & Beyond: Can Ecology and Commerce Co-exist?," *Ode Magazine*, March 8, 2007. www.organicconsumers.org/articles/article_4457.cfm.

53. Quoted in Kristen Collins, "Organic Food Goes Corporate," *The News & Observer*, March 29, 2007. www.newsobserver.com/102/ story/549685.html.

54. Goodall, *Harvest for Hope: A Guide to Mindful Eating*, p. 164.

55. Quoted in Kristen Collins, "Organic Food Goes Corporate," *The News & Observer*, March 29, 2007. www.newsobserver.com/102/ story/549685.html.

56. Center for Food Safety, "Organic and Beyond," undated. www. centerforfoodsafety.org/organic_an.cfm.

57. Organic Consumers Association, "SOS: Safeguard Organic Standards," 2006. www.organicconsumers.org/sos.cfm.

58. Quoted in Paula Lavigne, "Is Organic the Real Deal?," *Dallas Morning News*, July 17, 2006. www.dallasnews.com/sharedcontent/dws/dn/latestnews/stories/071606dnccoorganics.19c550e. html.

59. Organic Consumers Association, "Boycott the Shameless Seven— Organic Outlaws Labeling Factory Farm Milk as 'SDA Organic,'" March 29, 2007. www.democracyinaction.org/dia/organizationsORG/oca/campaign.jsp?campaign_KEY=4756.

60. Quoted in Stephen Leahy, "Environment: An Organic Recipe for Development," *Inter Press Service News Agency*, December 18, 2006. http://ipsnews.net/news.asp?idnews=35883.

61. Leahy, "Environment: An Organic Recipe for Development.

62. Leahy, "Environment: An Organic Recipe for Development.

DISCUSSION QUESTIONS

Chapter 1: The Meaning of "Organic"

1. What types of substances do the USDA organic regulations prohibit for use in producing organic foods?

2. What is the difference between "USDA Organic" foods and "natural" foods?

3. Describe some of the differences between organic farming methods and conventional farming methods.

Chapter 2: The Rise of the Organic Food Movement

1. According to the author, when did chemical-based, industrial farming begin in the United States? What events or historical developments contributed to its acceptance?

2. What famous book published in the 1960s helped to launch the environmental movement and increase consumer interest in organically grown foods?

3. When was the Organic Foods Production Act (OFPA) passed by Congress? When were the final organic regulations implemented by the U.S. government?

Chapter 3: Are There Health Benefits to Eating Organic?

1. According to organic advocates, what are the alleged dangers of non-organic foods? What are the health benefits of eating organically grown foods, according to these organic supporters?

2. Does the U.S. government take a position on whether organic food is safer than non-organic food?

3. What are some of the health risks of organically grown foods,

according to detractors?

Chapter 4: Organic Farming, The Environment, and Society

1. How does organic farming help the environment, according to the views of organic supporters?

2. What are the ways in which organic farming can harm the environment, according to its critics?

3. Describe the competing views in the current debate about whether organic farms can produce yields similar to conventional farms.

Chapter 5: The Future of Organic Food Production

1. According to the author, why are many organic supporters concerned about large corporations entering the organic industry?

2. According to the author, what is the "beyond organic" movement?

3. According to the book, why are some developing countries embracing organic food production methods?

Center for Food Safety

660 Pennsylvania Ave, SE, #302, Washington, D.C. 20003

Ph: (202)547-9359 _ Fax: (202)547-9429

Email: office@centerforfoodsafety.org

Web site: www.centerforfoodsafety.org/

The Center for Food Safety (CFS) is a non-profit public interest and environmental advocacy membership organization that seeks to challenge harmful food production technologies and promote sustainable alternatives. CFS uses various strategies, including litigation and legal advocacy, as well as public education, grassroots organizing, and media outreach. The CFS Web site contains topical information about a variety of organic and food-related issues, as well as links to numerous CFS publications. CFS also publishes a quarterly newsletter, called Food Safety Now!.

Environmental Working Group (EWG)

1436 U Street NW, Suite 100, Washington, D.C. 20009

Ph: (202) 667-6982 _ Fax: (202)232-2592

Web site: www.ewg.org/

The Environmental Working Group (EWG) is a non-profit, non-partisan public interest group dedicated to protecting public health and the environment. EWG's team of scientists, engineers, policy experts, lawyers, and computer programmers study government data, legal documents, scientific research and conduct their own laboratory tests to expose threats to public health and the environment, and to find solutions to those problems. The EWG Web site contains a wealth of information and in-depth reports about pesticides and other toxins in the environment, their effects on the human body, and issues affecting U.S. government organic standards, among other issues.

Center for Global Food Issues (CGFI)

P.O. Box 202, Churchville, VA 24421-0202

Ph: (540)337-6354 _ Fax: (540)337-8593

Email: cgfi@hughes.net _ Web site: www.cgfi.org/

The Center for Global Food Issues (CGFI) is a project of the Hudson Institute, a non-partisan policy research organization dedicated to promoting global security, prosperity, and freedom. CGFI conducts research and analysis on agriculture and environmental concerns, and seeks to promote free trade, support for technological innovations in agriculture, and awareness of how agricultural productivity is beneficial to environmental conservation. The group's Web site contains links to a number of publications criticizing organic farming.

The National Organic Program (NOP)

Rm. 4008-South Bldg., 1400 Independence Ave., S.W., Washington, D.C. 20250-0020
Ph: (202) 720-3252 _ Fax: (202) 205-7808
Web site: www.ams.usda.gov/nop/indexNet.htm

This is the Web site for the U.S. government's organic program. The site provides information for consumers, farmers, and the public about government organic standards and labeling. U.S. organic regulations are available here as well as other publications about the government's organic program.

Organic Consumers Association (OCA)

6771 South Silver Hill Drive, Finland MN 55603
Ph: (218)226-4164 _ Fax: (218)353-7652
Web site: http://www.organicconsumers.org/

The Organic Consumers Association (OCA) is a grassroots, non-profit public interest organization that campaigns for health, justice, and sustainable agriculture. The OCA works to maintain strict U.S. organic standards and to promote the interests of organic consumer on a wide variety of issues, including food safety, genetic engineering, children's health, corporate accountability, fair trade, the environment. The OCA's Web site contains information and recent news about many of these issues, as well as links to other publications and organic organizations.

Organic Trade Association (OTA)

P.O. Box 547, Greenfield, MA 01302
Ph: (413)774-7511 _ Fax: (413)774-6432
Email: info@ota.com _ Website: www.ota.com/index.html

The Organic Trade Association (OTA) is a membership business association for the organic industry in North America. OTA seeks to promote and protect organic trade to benefit the environment, farmers, the public, and the economy. Its Web site contains information about the industry, organic standards, the benefits of organic food, and recent organic-related news. The OTA also publishes a newsletter, What's News in Organics, and maintains a Web site for consumers called "The O'Mama Report," (www.theorganicreport.com/).

FOR MORE INFORMATION

Books

Alex Avery, *The Truth About Organic Foods*, St. Louis, MO: Henderson Communications, 2006. A science-based analysis critical of many claims of organic food advocates and supportive of more affordable, conventionally grown foods.

Rachel Carson, *Silent Spring*, Wilmington, Boston, MA: Houghton Mifflin Co., 1962. A compelling, readable, and now famous indictment of chemical-based agriculture that is credited with launching the environmental movement.

Andrew Kimbrell, ed., *Fatal Harvest: The Tragedy of Industrial Agriculture*, Washington, D.C.: Island Press, 2002. A critical look at conventional agriculture based on health, environmental, and moral grounds.

Marion Nestle, *What to Eat*, New York: North Point Press, 2006. Geared towards helping consumers make sense of confusing information about our food, this author provides simple guidelines about what is healthy to eat, the marketing ploys of big food companies, and the meaning of complex food labels.

Peter Pringle. *Food, Inc.: Mendel to Monsanto—the Promises and Perils of the Biotech Harvest*, New York: Simon & Schuster, 2003. A journalist's view of the negative effects of biotechnology and corporate control on the world's food supply.

Michael Pollan, *The Omnivore's Dilemma: a Natural History of Four Meals*, New York: Penguin Press, 2006. This book examines how our food is grown and the consequences of everyday food choices, both for ourselves and for the environment.

Peter Singer and Jim Mason, *The Way We Eat: Why Our Food Choices Matter*, Emmaus, PA: Rodale, 2006. A review of our food choices, such as organic versus non-organic and vegetarianism versus meat-eating, and the accompanying ethical, moral, and practical effects of those choices.

Periodicals

Diane Brady, "The Organic Myth; Pastoral Ideals Are Getting Trampled as Organic Food Goes Mass Market," *Business Week*, October 16, 2006, Iss. 4005, p. 50.

Brian Halweil, "Can Organic Farming Feed Us All?," *World Watch*, May 1, 2006.

Anna Kuchment, "Food: What's on Your Label?," *Newsweek*, March 12, 2007. www.thegreenguide.com/docprint.mhtml? i=gginnews&s=newsweek0307.

Field Maloney, "Is Whole Foods Wholesome? The Dark Secrets of the Organic-Food Movement," *Slate*, March 17, 2006. www.slate.com/id/2138176/.

Reed Mangels, "Health Benefits of Organic Food for Children," *Vegetarian Journal*, May-June 2006, Vol. 25, Iss. 3, p. 12.

Jason Mark, "Food Fight: Is the 'Organic' Label Being Amended to Uselessness?," *Earth Island Journal*, Spring 2006, Vol. 21, Iss. 1, p. 44.

Websites

Organic Trade Association, "The O'Mama Report" (www.theor-ganicreport.com/). An on-line resource about organic agriculture and organic products for consumers, containing recipes, activity ideas for children, and gardening tips. It is run by the Organic Trade Association, the association for the organic industry in North America.

U.S. Environmental Protection Agency (EPA), "Organic Farming," (www.epa.gov/oecaagct/torg.html). A government Web site that provides an overview of the U.S. organic program and standards, with links to related agricultural topics, such as sustainability, pesticides, and preventing pollution.

PICTURE CREDITS

ABOUT THE AUTHOR

Debra A. Miller is a writer and lawyer with a passion for current events and history. She began her law career in Washington, D.C., where she worked on legislative, policy, and legal matters in government, public interest, and private law firm positions. She now lives with her husband in Encinitas, California. She has written and edited numerous books and anthologies on historical, political, health, and other topics.